Let's Talk REACH

Let's Talk
REACH

James Garratt

T

Copyright © 2024 James Garratt

The moral right of the author has been asserted.

Apart from any fair dealing for the purposes of research or private study, or criticism or review, as permitted under the Copyright, Designs and Patents Act 1988, this publication may only be reproduced, stored or transmitted, in any form or by any means, with the prior permission in writing of the publishers, or in the case of reprographic reproduction in accordance with the terms of licences issued by the Copyright Licensing Agency. Enquiries concerning reproduction outside those terms should be sent to the publishers.

Troubador Publishing Ltd
Unit E2 Airfield Business Park,
Harrison Road, Market Harborough,
Leicestershire. LE16 7UL
Tel: 0116 2792299
Email: books@troubador.co.uk
Web: www.troubador.co.uk/matador
Twitter: @matadorbooks

ISBN 978 1805143 550

British Library Cataloguing in Publication Data.
A catalogue record for this book is available from the British Library.

Printed and bound in the UK by TJ Books Limited, Padstow, Cornwall
Typeset in 13pt Bradley Hand ITC by Troubador Publishing Ltd, Leicester, UK

So, what's it all about?

It's not about our whereabouts, or even in-between.

It's not about grand plans, or unrealistic schemes.

It's just about the component parts that make life what it is.

It's about sorting out our R, E, A, C, H, which determine how we live.

INTRODUCTION

I'm kind of assuming, because you have started to read this book, that you are intrigued by the title: Let's talk REACH.

But even if you understand, **what we are supposed to be talking about**, your next thought would probably be: **how can we possibly do this** (have a conversation, that is) through the pages of a book? Well, let me explain.

What I will be **assuming**, as I write this book, are **the kind of questions** that you (or someone else) **could** or **might ask**, and **the kind of comments** that you (or someone else) **could** or **might make**, related to **the topics in question**, at the time.

And just to make it clear, when you are speaking (as it were) I will use orange text, otherwise things could get confusing.

And just in case you are still confused about what we are supposed to be talking about (which you probably aren't, because you have worked it out from the front cover) let me explain the use of the word REACH:

REACH is an acronym, and the letters **R, E, A, C** and **H** are the first letters of the words: **R**elationships, **E**njoyment, **A**chievements, **C**omfort and **H**ealth.

But why are these 'words' important?

Now we're talking!

Because, in my opinion, **R**elationships, **E**njoyment, **A**chievements, **C**omfort and **H**ealth are **the basic ingredients of human life**.

The basic ingredients of human life?

Let's talk REACH

Yes, think about it. Think about **anything** you have ever experienced in your life, or are ever likely to experience, and I'm sure you will discover that **whatever you thought about**, will have, or would be related to one or more of these areas.

Go on.

Life, for most people, is a roller coaster of ups and downs, spells of good luck and misfortune (yes?) and some of the time, we have to accept that this is, just life.

Some of the time?

Of course. Some things are beyond our influence, beyond our control. Throughout history (and that includes the here and now) the thinking and behaviour of **some individuals** has had (and continues to have) consequences for millions of other people.

Sometimes **their thinking** and **behaviour** has resulted in **positive benefits**, of course, but in some cases, the **consequences** have been, and continue to be, **extremely negative.**

But, for you and me (ordinary individuals, living ordinary sorts of lives) could, I suggest, with a little more effort and thought, improve our own lives, and those with whom we relate, today. After all, we are **social animals**; life revolves around other people and within our **R, E, A, C** and **H** situations – and just as **other people's behaviour can affect us**, so **our behaviour can affect them.**

I understand that.

Life itself can create a multitude of different **challenges** and **opportunities**, which can impact on our very existence, and we don't necessarily have to just accept things as they are, we can take control, and have an impact, ourselves.

INTRODUCTION

So, to begin to get our minds around some of life's **R**, **E**, **A**, **C** and **H** situations, let's read a poem entitled, **Life Is**.

Sorry, I forgot to tell you. I use poems quite a lot throughout this book, just simple poems, not 'Wordsworth' or 'Tennyson'. Easy to read poems that help to get across the messages as we proceed, and if useful, allow the information to stick in the mind. I hope you are OK with that.

Life Is

Everyday should ideally be an adventure in your life, but it might not seem that way in the morning when we rise.

Some demands, the difficult ones, can affect our peace of mind, with consequences for our own well-being, and other people's lives.

But it really shouldn't be this way, life has so much to offer, and it's up to us to get it right, we can't rely on others to bother.

Life, you see, is a special gift, and at birth you received that prize, and being here at all, no less, did not on ourselves rely.

Millions of sperm you see, battled to reach an awaiting egg, so is life very special, or is it a burden around your neck?

I do realise, that whilst **life is undoubtably a special gift**, for those who are suffering as a result of stress, anxiety, pain, disadvantage, disability, abuse, prejudice, mental ill health, and so on, life may not seem that special.

There are so many different 'Issues' in life that can affect any of our **R**, **E**, **A**, **C** and **H** situations, and at different times of our lives, too.

Let's talk REACH

There are **some things** over which we have **no control** (obviously) and maybe, we just have to accept these. But there are **other things** in life, over which we most definitely **should be able to have some control**.

Sometimes **having control** over life's events, situations and experiences, can be down to the way we think, and what we think about.

Put it this way:

The way we think, and what we think about, affects the way we feel, and the way we feel has the potential to affect:

- Our **relationships** (personal and professional).
- Our **enjoyment** of life.
- Our **achievements** in life.
- Life's **comforts**.
- Our **health** (both mental and physical).

Thoughts are fine, and absolutely essential for life (obviously), but when our **thoughts** have a **negative impact** on **life's situations**, then **thinking differently** may well be what's required to enable us to 'sort things out', not only for our own well-being, but for the benefit and well-being of those with whom we relate.

Thinking differently! What do you mean?

Well, if you accept that the way we think, and what we think about affects the way we feel, and that the way we feel has consequences, for any, or all of our **R, E, A, C** and **H** situations, then clearly **those thought processes, may need to change.** In other words, **we may need to think differently.**

INTRODUCTION

Without thought, human activity (as we know it) would not exist because thought (the processing of information in the mind) is the initiator of the emotional and physical responses that drive human activity. But thinking is a hugely complex topic so, let's begin our thinking by reading the following poem entitled, **It's in the Mind**.

It's in the Mind

Thoughts are sensations in the mind, of images and silent sound.

Sometimes questions, answers too, sometimes knowing what to say or do. Sometimes feeling, right or wrong. Sometimes feeling weak or strong.

Conversations in our heads that can often leave us full of dread, and past experiences that can cloud the mind, with tormented, twisted sounds and sight.

But if our thoughts can be inspired by wholesome consequences and desires then not just ourselves, but others too, should benefit from the way we think and what we think about and do.

And since thoughts often precede what happens next (another thought or life event), thinking is a skill to nurture, to ensure the best, for everybody's future.

We live busy lives, and most of the time we don't give much thought to our **moment-by-moment thinking** (do we?) and impatience, intolerance, and a multitude of other behavioural characteristics can have a significant impact on our lives. The things we say, and the things we do, sometimes take place without much **forethought**, and things can go wrong.

Go wrong?

Let's talk REACH

Yes, an individual's responses may not be quite what we had expected, and we end up putting our foot in it ourselves (so to speak).

The word **forethought** is interesting in this context because we have to bear in mind that we have **a conscious mind** and **a subconscious mind**.

The conscious mind responds, moment-by-moment, to the 'information' **received via the senses of sight, sound, touch, taste and smell**, whilst the subconscious mind **'refers to' information stored in our memory**, the result of past experiences, and so on.

This cocktail of information, provided by our senses, our past experiences, our opinions, ideas, attitudes and beliefs, can all have a powerful influence on our very being.

And this is why I am proposing that we should have this conversation, because **being us** has the potential for both good, and the opposite, in all its extremes.

I do not profess to be an expert in any of the topics discussed in this book. My aim, whilst having this conversation, is to encourage you (and myself) **to think differently about things**, sometimes. To consider different points of view, to think about the consequences of our own actions (if needs be), to think about other people's behaviours and their consequences. Indeed, to think about anything that could potentially make our own and other people's lives better: happier, less stressful, and more fulfilling.

With all of the above in mind, and whilst recognising that our **R, E, A, C** and **H** experiences are often interrelated, it can be useful, for clarity, to consider each area separately.

So, let's make a start with the chapter **R for Relationships**.

OK, sounds 'interesting' – so, let's go for it.

R for Relationships

Relationships are the **fabric of life**, and it is around relationships, of every kind, that our entire lives revolve. But let's consider for a while, **interpersonal relationships**.

Relationship building, is a lifelong process, and the **characteristics**, **abilities** and **qualities** that an individual **brings to the process**, as a result of **learning**, **experiences** and **thought**, are the **building blocks**, upon which relationships develop.

People engage in personal relationships for lots of different reasons…

Obviously.

And some of which are 'spoken about' in the following poem entitled, **Relationships**.

Relationships

Relationships have a purpose, that's why, of course, they exist. To communicate and exchange emotions, quite often tops of the list.

Companionship is what we gain, to have an enjoyable time, and sometimes just to help us to unwind and discuss what's on our minds.

To share and discuss opinions, ideas and points of view, is often why we engage with others, to sort out what to do.

Sometimes relationships result in romantic ties, with a lifelong bond, with children and family life and planning years beyond.

And then there are those relationships with the growing kids, and this we really must get right; their future depends on this.

Let's talk REACH

Not least, we relate to those we hardly know, in all sorts of situations, but for those involved, these can create all sorts of complications.

Whilst relationships can satisfy all sorts of needs and wants (as the poem suggests), **relationships can fail**, and for lots of different reasons.

Sometimes, when a relationship fails, **it's our own fault**. Sometimes **it's someone else's fault**, and sometimes **it's just circumstances**.

And sometimes you're not quite sure what went wrong and the consequences are not nice!

True – and the poem below illustrates how (for example) **loneliness** and **distress** can be the consequences of a relationship failure.

Loneliness

Friendships are relationships, a very special part of human life, but when things go wrong, which they sometimes do, you're left feeling quite deprived.

The loss of a friend can leave you very isolated and the resulting feeling, loneliness, can leave you quite disorientated.

Was it me or was it them; I need to have some answers. If it was me, I need to know what caused their dissatisfaction.

But often it doesn't work like this; you're left floundering in the dark, and loneliness can cause such pain, without you knowing how it came about.

R for Relationships

To cap it all, and make things worse, the vultures may begin to circle, to bully, abuse or discriminate. Whatever suits their purpose.

And this is when someone on whom you can rely could help you to survive, to be there and support you and to stand right by your side.

We all need someone to take an interest and to listen to our woes, to laugh and even cry with and to share what each other knows.

So, to all concerned, the message is: when circumstances arise, always do your best to alleviate suffering in other people's lives.

And try to avoid behaviours that could torment another's mind, because you never know when things could turn around, and you could be the one who's down.

We all know the importance of friendships, and I agree; they are indeed a special part of human life.

Companionship is so important – we all need someone to relate to, to chat to, to share our concerns with, to plan activities with, to laugh with, to cry with, and if appropriate, to be romantic with. In other words, to share and experience life with. But things do go wrong, and sometimes the fault is ours.

You are absolutely right, and as the poem reminds us:

...avoid behaviours that could torment another's mind, because you never know when things could turn around, and you could be the one that's down.

It's in situations like the above, that **self-awareness** can be so valuable.

Let's talk REACH

Self-awareness?

Yes. Self-awareness is being aware of how our inclinations, characteristics and normal behaviours can affect other people's feelings, as well as our own.

And becoming more self-aware may require us to ask ourselves some tough questions. For example:

Do we like ourselves?

There's a good chance that our answer will be either:

Yes, I do like myself.

Or, if we're not quite sure:

I think I like myself.

But, if things have not been going too well recently, for any number of reasons, some might say:

No, I don't really like myself.

If we can answer, **'yes, I do like myself'**, or, **'I think I like myself'**, and it was **for the right reasons**, then that's a great start. But who am I to tell anyone what the right reasons are?

Well, I can only suggest that if you enjoy hurting people, abusing people, upsetting people, cheating on people, stealing from people, or taking advantage of people in any way, then these are not ideal reasons for liking oneself.

But for anyone reading this book who (at the moment) doesn't really like themselves (for whatever reasons) then what I would say is this: read on and things hopefully will change, and you might begin to feel differently, and even decide to change some of your behaviour.

R for Relationships

Anyway, for the moment, let's assume that we do like ourselves because we think we are quite nice people. This kind of implies that **our moral values**, our personal views relating to 'right and wrong', must (to a certain extent) be based on the premise that 'other people matter' and this is in our minds, **when relating to others**.

I'll go along with that.

And let's be clear, relating to others and reacting to life's demands is, or should be, **a natural developmental process**, ensuring that **our mind, abilities and skills match life's constantly changing demands and expectations**.

Of course, and this might require us to make circumstantial changes, and/or personal changes.

Absolutely, and this is why becoming more **self-aware**, is so important. We might **think we know ourselves**, and some people have a very high opinion of themselves, but how well do we actually know ourselves?

The thing about people is: we are all so very different and, like it or not, we can be advantaged, or not, by the kind of **personality traits** listed below, and to which we might not even be fully aware.

So, you might like to ask yourself these questions. Am I:

An optimist **or** a pessimist.

Confident **or** reserved.

Generous **or** selfish.

Quiet **or** loud.

Sensitive **or** brash.

Let's talk REACH

Just a minute. It's not possible to give a specific answer to this question. Different circumstances can result in different responses; you can't be optimistic, or confident, for example, in all situations.

I agree. But being aware of any **'deficiencies'** (if that's what they are) may only come to mind if we are prepared to **put in an effort to become more self-aware**, or, if someone else brings them to our attention.

There are, of course, many other **'characteristics'** that can **advantage** or **disadvantage** us in our relationships and in life in general. With this in mind, look at the lists below, and ask yourself this question: **Which of these apply to me? Am I:**

Considerate – Lazy – Reliable – Humble – **Impatient** – Gentle – Dominant – Compassionate – Aggressive – Caring – Kind – Negative – Arrogant – Loving – Honest – **Intolerant** – Unreliable – and so on.

Notice that I have emboldened **impatient** and **intolerant** in the above list. Whilst these are only two of any number of 'negative' behavioural characteristics (that do us no favours) you will discover, as you read on, that these characteristics can have a significant impact in some people's lives and in all sorts of situations.

OK, I can't dispute this – but this is getting rather personal.

Maybe – but the better we know ourselves, and, if necessary, are prepared to change, then chances are, this will result in a happier and more fulfilling life.

I do accept, of course, that many people who struggle with life's challenges **may not have the ability, energy, support** or **mental health** to enable them to make the effort needed to behave differently **even if they wanted to**.

R for Relationships

Life can be difficult for a multitude of reasons and **we are unique individuals**. We are all different, and those differences can affect how we live our lives, and how we respond to life's challenges, including how we conduct ourselves within our relationships.

But this 'uniqueness' can be the result of our **childhood experiences** (positive and negative) and as adults, whilst we might acknowledge the above, **we may not even be aware of some of the factors**, within our own childhood experiences, **that could have influenced 'who we have become'** and how this could be affecting our lives.

Childhood experiences will almost certainly have impacted on **the way we think** and **what we think about**, and **how we think** has **consequences**. Not least our thinking can impact on our self-esteem and confidence, the way we relate to and treat others, and even how successful we become in our life pursuits and to some extent even our health.

In this context, read the following poem that makes some suggestions related to our **thinking**, and in particular, **first thoughts**.

First Thoughts

Have you ever thought about how your thoughts first started out? Did you form them on your own? No, thoughts are rarely yours alone.

Life dictates how thoughts are formed and, in your memory, some are stored. So even when your thoughts seem clear, your mind can sometimes be elsewhere.

The conscious mind is at your service, and through the senses provides awareness. But in darkness dwells the subconscious mind, where memories can lurk and hide.

Let's talk REACH

So, your thoughts are not necessarily due, to what you see, or hear, or do. Let's be clear, it might sound scary, but of your thoughts, you must be wary.

The subconscious mind, without even showing, can influence your thoughts without you knowing.

But don't get down, don't feel deflated, you're not a robot, you're a human creation. With a little effort and determination, you can make the right interpretations.

So, what is this poem suggesting?

Firstly, that: Thoughts are rarely yours alone.

And: Life dictates how thoughts are formed, and in your memory, some are stored.

The problem is, some of life's experiences, memories and emotions, **can become so ingrained in our memory**, that even, with the development of **independent thinking** (as we mature) they can have **a powerful effect on our very being**, and often for many years into the future.

The following poem, entitled **Childhood Memories**, illustrates how different childhood experiences could (potentially) impact on a child's later life.

Childhood Memories

Early childhood memories (the ones you have), were they good or were they bad?

My first memories start at five: adventures and laughs; such happy times.

R for Relationships

At five I remember having to go away, to be with Gran for a couple of days.

My grandparents made our lives such fun: treats and treasures for everyone.

Gran said Mum and Dad had to sort things out, but I didn't understand what it was all about.

I bet they were planning something nice; Mum and Dad were always arranging for us a surprise.

No! later Gran said things hadn't gone to plan, and when I got back home, Dad had gone.

When you got back home your dad had gone, I'm sorry to hear that, was he away for long?

He never returned. It was just me and Mum, and that's how it was until I was ten.

How did that make you feel? To me it would have felt very surreal.

It wasn't nice. Mum did her best, but times were tough and she had little rest.

I remember it well: a busy home. Can't imagine Mum doing everything all on her own.

I helped a lot, I grew up fast, but it affected my schoolwork, homework and tests.

I'm sorry to hear that you had such bad luck. It sounds like your early life was really quire tough.

Let's talk REACH

The **early years of childhood development** should be **a time of great opportunity**; an opportunity enhanced by the quality of the children's interactions with their family members, other people, their environment, and even other creatures.

But unfortunately, childhood experiences can be very different. Children will experience different circumstances, different opportunities, different everything, and these 'differences' **can** have a significant impact on their future lives.

For some, childhood experiences can cause all sorts of problems. For others, they can provide a great character-building experience. The following poem raises a few more questions on the subject.

Is Life Fair?

Do we all have equal wealth?

Do we all have perfect health?

Do we all have self-respect?

Do we all, our looks, accept?

Do we all have equal minds?

Do we all have the same good times?

Do we all have others in our lives to share?

Do we all have the same capacity to love and care?

Is life fair? No, it's not. So, what do we do; give up and accept our lot?

No! Do not despair, don't allow your lot in life to become a lifetime snare.

R for Relationships

There are so many different 'issues' in life, that have the potential to drag us down, and this can apply to anyone of any age, and yes, we may, as a result, **feel despair**.

But **despair is so destructive on many different fronts**; it clouds the thinking, distorts emotions, and can result in all sorts of inappropriate, or unhelpful, behaviours. Behaviours which can affect family life, friendships, partner relationships, colleagues, and so on.

But as stated in the poem **First thoughts**:

But don't get down, don't feel deflated, you're not a robot, you're a human creation.

With a little effort and determination, you can make the right interpretations.

This is all very well if we can do it; make the right interpretations. But how do we know what the right interpretations are? If being us (as you put it) is, to some extent, down to other people's influences, and the experiences which other people have created for us, to what extent is being us, down to us?

Well, the answer to this is partly as follows. As we mature, we develop **the ability to think for ourselves** and come to our own conclusions most of the time.

What do you mean – most of the time?

Well, we do have to bear in mind that the **subconscious mind** (referred to in the poem First Thought) does have a role to play in our lives. And why? Because it (the subconscious mind) has access to past experiences, images and emotions (stored in our memory) which it can use (if we allow it), **to influence our conscious thinking** and **behaviour**.

Let's talk REACH

In this context, the following poem makes a few references to 'past experience', which, if not thought about and addressed, can have consequences. The poem is entitled, **Mislead**.

Mislead

So here we are. We've made it so far. We're adults now and the future is ours.

To make the best of what we have become, or else prove that the doubters had got it all wrong.

To prove that we have more than we dared to expect, and to show to some others that they were, in fact, incorrect.

Or else we'll just leave things exactly as they are; that's the easy way out, it's how we've survived so far.

But no, that's not right. I don't want to feel this way. I can do it and I think I can do it my way.

It'll take some effort. I might get things wrong, but I'll try my very best, and I'll do what I can.

The person speaking in this poem has started to engage in **self-analysis**, and as a result is becoming more **self-aware**. Not least they have come to realise that their **lack of confidence** may not necessarily be their fault.

Furthermore, they have made the decision to 'try to put things right' and to put in the effort necessary, to make the progress of which they believe they are capable.

R for Relationships

Self-awareness is a **valuable asset**, because **'being us'** and **knowing how this might affect others** with whom we relate, is hugely important.

And whilst you might be very confident and self-aware, chances are there will be someone you know, who doesn't feel that way, and you may be able to help them.

Lack of self-awareness can have negative consequences in all sorts of situations, and in particular, in one's personal relationships.

One of the individuals referred to in the following poem most certainly lacks self-awareness, which has resulted in a very upsetting situation. It's entitled, **Critical Disclosure**.

Critical Disclosure

Nobody likes to have their intelligence questioned, their ability to think things through; to apply skills and knowledge to work out what to say or do.

So, if someone criticises your emotional intelligence, it can be quite disturbing. Especially if you fancy that someone and their comments might be deserving.

What you lack (they said) is self-awareness, and emotional intelligence demands its service.

It's knowing how your inclinations, characteristics and normal behaviours affects the way others are feeling.

But you don't get it, you seem oblivious to what your behaviour is revealing.

I'm sorry (they said) but I've had enough; you've made my life a misery. I don't want to see you anymore; I need to start my recovery.

Let's talk REACH

Clearly, the individual speaking in the above poem received **a critical disclosure** that probably came as a huge shock. Chances are they would have felt embarrassed, distraught and presumably unhappy about the disclosure.

Alternatively, they may have felt angry and insulted and not able to accept such criticism.

I agree, but in either case, their sense of well-being is likely to have been affected.

The individual who decided **that they had had enough** and chose **to walk away**, had probably spent a lot of time with the prospective future partner, only to realise that his or her behaviour, attitudes, selfishness, or whatever, had made them feel uneasy, uncomfortable, fearful even, which could have a lasting effect on their sense of well-being.

Both individuals in this situation **are victims**, victims **of issues that have the potential to affect their mental health.**

So, what's going on? What is 'whoever' being accused of?

Well, line three of the poem appears to have the answer. It states:

What you lack (they said) is self-awareness, and emotional intelligence demands its service.

Emotional intelligence?

Yes. **Emotional intelligence** is having an understanding of **how** our inclinations, characteristics, normal behaviours and emotions can affect the emotions of others. But also, **having the ability to manage those characteristics** whilst being empathetically aware of the feelings of others.

R for Relationships

So, the individual in the poem is being accused of not having a conscious awareness of their own inclinations, characteristics, behaviours and emotions, and thereby, not being aware of the consequential impact.

Correct – and in this connection, can I remind you of the question I asked earlier: **Do we like ourselves?**

And if you remember, it was suggested that **if we think we do** (like ourselves) then this kind of implies that **our moral values**, our personal views relating to 'right and wrong', must (to a certain extent) be based on the premise **that 'other people matter'**. And if we believe that other people matter, then being aware of how our behaviours are likely to affect others (with whom we relate) is so important.

But, as we go about our busy lives, considering whether we like ourselves is not something we tend to think about very often.

I suppose not. In fact, self-awareness often only happens when our behaviour is brought into question, as illustrated in the above poem. In this example, it was negative feedback, but positive feedback can be valuable too.

What we need to understand, and remember, is that **self-awareness** requires **self-analysis**.

Sometimes we are **forced to do this** (self-analyse) as a result of other people's comments, or reactions, alternatively we may do this 'voluntarily' by just **thinking** (having a conversation with ourselves, in our heads).

If we could all do this more frequently (try to become more self-aware), then we might be better prepared to deal with life's challenges as they arise and make 'better' choices sometimes. What do you think?

Let's talk REACH

I can't really dispute that.

In this context, the following poem, entitled, **Self-awareness**, has a few things to say on the subject.

Self-awareness

What makes me who I am and to whom should I compare? But why am I having these thoughts at all; why should I even care?

The answer, I'm told, is not that simple. Because there are many implications and failing to have self-awareness, they say, can create all sorts of complications.

Not least, what I do suggest or say, can impact on other people's reactions. But why should I be concerned, if my behaviour is to my satisfaction?

Fair enough, they say, if you don't care about what other people think or do. But make no mistake, if your behaviour affects them, it will almost certainly affect you too.

So, let's get this straight. What you're telling me, is that 'being me' has implications. The way I live, and how I am, can affect my own and other people's situations.

Lack of self-awareness, you suggest, can make one quite dysfunctional, and this can affect other people's lives, and make them feel uncomfortable.

OK, OK, I see your point; self-analysis is the key. Because having self-awareness is good for all – yes, OK, including me.

So, if I can interact with others without having a negative impact on their lives, I might be able to say to myself, 'I'm doing fine'. No more thoughts may be required.

R for Relationships

But if, in my interactions, I can enhance other's people's lives, then I might be able to say to myself, 'That's good; I'm now helping others to feel alright'.

So, this is self-awareness, yes? The result of self-analysis. So, to get things right, to sort things out, I need to clear my mind's paralysis?

Mind's paralysis?

Absolutely, and in this context, **paralysis** suggests being unable to respond empathetically to the feelings and emotions of others.

And as the following line from the poem suggests, self-analysis may be what's required:

OK, OK, I see your point; self-analysis is the key, because having self-awareness is good for all – yes, OK, including me.

At this point, it would be appropriate, I think, to introduce to the concept of the four Cs:

The four Cs?

Yes. **C**ommunication, **C**ompassion, **C**ompromise and **C**ommitment, which, in my opinion, are the most basic requirements of successful personal relationships.

Effective **communication** is so important, but it only happens when those involved feel equally confident about expressing their opinions, and where a disagreement (if it occurs) can be resolved with amicable discussion. Shouting or becoming aggressive, or at the other extreme, not speaking or communicating, does little to enhance a relationship.

Let's talk REACH

That's all very well, but if you are tired, had a bad day at work, and so on, it's very easy to 'lose it' and say the wrong things.

Very true. Situations happen which can cause an individual to feel anxious or upset, angry even – and this is where **self-control** is so important. After all, it's in everybody's interests for our interpersonal relationships to be amicable.

Furthermore, poor adult behaviour is far from ideal for any **children in the home. Children learn by example**, and they are learning **moment by moment**. Parenting is an ongoing process and as the years pass by, all sorts of 'influences' including: the media, peers, and so on, have to be 'accommodated' by the parents. Being a parent is a hugely responsible job.

And then there's **compassion**. Compassion is a response that one individual makes to another **where suffering or anxiety is effectively shared**. This is particularly important in close, interpersonal relationships because mutual concern and respect is the bedrock of stable and successful relationships.

I agree, but you do have to be careful when it comes to compassion.

As honourable as compassion is in a personal relationship, you do have to be careful that you do not allow yourself to be 'tricked' (by someone else's disguised suffering, distress or disappointment) into a situation that disadvantages you. It can happen, even in a stable interpersonal relationship.

Good point. I totally accept this.

And what about **compromise**? We all have **our own likes and dislikes, wants and needs**, but when we relate to others, **compromise** is so important. Compromise ensures that those involved are comfortable with the outcome of any decisions made, or actions that need to be taken. Everyone needs to feel that their views or opinions are being

R for Relationships

taken into consideration and not being 'sidelined' in any way or ignored.

I agree with this.

Commitment is essential **to ensure that trust is maintained at 'every level'**. Commitment to each other is fundamental to maintaining a long-term, successful relationship. If commitment seems to be in doubt (at any time), alarm bells will inevitably start ringing.

We've made some very good points in relation to the four Cs. But to achieve any or all of the above, empathy is required; which the following poem explains quite well.

Empathy Revealed

Empathy's a funny word unless you know its meaning. So, let's give it some thought, to see what it's revealing?

It's all about what others are thinking, their emotions and their feelings. But they're not always easy to read, in fact they can be quite concealing.

But let's be clear; we are not just talking here about our keen perceptions, our ability to recognise other's feelings and emotions in different situations.

It's about a deeper recognition where our opinion doesn't count, but rather where their point of view is what it's all about.

So, empathy demands our minds be completely clear and open to the way others view and experience their personal situations.

And because we're social animals and benefit from joint respect, empathy, if wisely employed, should help all concerned achieve their best.

Let's talk REACH

But it's not always easy (I know) to see ourselves as we actually are, or as other people see us, or to understand that our behaviour might affect others in unintentional ways on occasions.

That's true.

So, unless **you are sure** that **being you, is the best you can be**, for your own well-being, and the well-being of those with whom you interreact, then maybe **having a conversation with yourself**, related to some of the questions on pages 11 and 12, could be useful.

A conversation with myself!

Yes. Ask yourself these questions again: Am I an optimist or a pessimist? Am I confident or shy? Am I generous or selfish? – and so on. And, am I considerate, reliable, gentle and compassionate? Or, am I, lazy, impatient, dominant, negative? And so on.

In answering these questions; you might have nothing negative to say about yourself, and that would be great if it was completely true. But **none of us are perfect**, and this, I suppose, is where **the conscience** comes into play.

The conscience?

Yes, that inner voice which questions our thoughts and actions.

Whether you believe that **conscience** is the result of **the rational mind** making **moral decisions**, based on experiences and influences, or **the voice of God** prompting our actions – ultimately, how you respond is still up to you. But making the 'wrong decision' or taking the 'wrong course of action' resulting in your own, or someone else's discomfort or distress, is not good.

Clearly, having self-awareness (as discussed above) and having the will and ability to moderate our behaviour (if we need to) in the light

R for Relationships

of this awareness, should pay dividends in any, or all of our **R, E, A, C** and **H** experiences.

And with this in our mind, it might be appropriate (since we are talking about adult relationships) to give some thought to **intimate relationships**.

This is a hugely complex topic, when one considers **the very personal nature of such relationships**. So, I'm not going to take this any further, other than to say the following.

If you are the kind of person (male or female) for whom changing intimate partners regularly is your choice, then the concept of **commitment** (one of the four Cs) cannot be relevant to you.

If, however, your hope is to meet a long-term partner, with all the benefits that this **should** provide, including: security, enjoyment, happiness, less stress, a sense of well-being (in other words a general feeling of fulfilment) for yourself and your partner, and for any children that you may have, then **commitment** is hugely important.

Commitment: 'For better or worse, in sickness and in health' (as voiced in many marriage services), is a long-established and appropriate sentiment, I believe, and it applies equally to those who choose to live together, and never marry.

But commitment is a very interesting concept when it comes to relationships, because it can mean different things to different couples.

It certainly can. It is suggested, however (in some research), that individuals who have **a deep affection for one another** are more likely to sustain a long-term relationship because they have **the desire** and **abilities** to maintain the magic.

Well, yes, that's obvious.

Let's talk REACH

Having a **deep affection**, I suggest, has its foundations in the four Cs, but encapsulates, of course, a whole range of other mutually beneficial qualities, including **patience** and **tolerance** (referred to earlier), and which are 'spoken' about in the following poem, entitled, **Being Myself**.

Being Myself

Being myself, the person I am, can patience really be part of the plan? Can patience affect my relationships, how other people see me and how I interreact?

Of course, it can. What am I thinking about? Maybe it's time to sort myself out.

To understand my impatience, I need a have a plan. And to start the process, self-analysis is maybe the way that I can.

So, I need to ask some questions, and answer them in truth. Questions that reveal the source of the feelings that impatience can induce.

Do I get impatient because I'm intolerant of what others do, and do other people's way of life affect me through and through?

Do I get impatient because delays cause me distress, and if it does, is time the factor that I should probably address?

Is my impatience just intolerance, a selfish point of view, played out in haste to make sure that I achieve what I want to do?

Do I get impatient to put my views across, and do I think that I am always right and others clearly are not?

Maybe it's time to start thinking anew. I realise now, it's not all about me, it's also about others too.

R for Relationships

The person speaking in this poem is engaging in **self-analysis**...

There's a lot of self-analyses taking place on these pages! Sorry to interrupt.

That's OK. As a result of the **self-analysis**, the speaker is becoming more **self-aware** in relation **to their thought processes** and **how these might be affecting their behaviour** within their relationships.

But we all get impatient on occasions, don't we? Intolerant even. That's what living a busy life can do to you.

Maybe, but as we will discuss later, it's not particularly good for our health and it doesn't do others any favours either, including: family members, friends, work colleagues, partners, and even people you might relate to momentarily in a shop, on the street, whilst driving, and so on.

Some people, unfortunately, have the opinion that only their opinion is what matters; they have a right to their opinions and other people simply need to 'fall into line'.

Not an ideal way to think, in my opinion. The following poem, entitled, **Uniqueness**, illustrates the kind of thinking to which I refer.

Uniqueness

I'm an individual member of the human race, with my own feelings and my own tastes.

My own thoughts and points of view, my own knowing what to say or do.

My own interests, wants and needs; there's no one else I desire to please.

Let's talk REACH

My opinions, right or wrong, it's not something I dwell on for very long.

A member of the human race, with my own existence, my own space.

It's the way I am, and I feel OK, and actually I don't care about what others might say.

Whilst the individual speaking in the above poem might believe that they are completely justified in their 'self-centred' views, these attitudes have consequences. Not least, they will almost certainly **impact on their relationships**, because others will likely **become more intolerant of them.**

Certainly, when considering **romantic relationships**, this way of thinking has no place at all. This is reflected in the following poem which considers a more 'acceptable' way to behave.

Romantic Relationships

Relationships work at their best when those involved show due respect. Respect considers all points of view, and compromise determines what to do.

Romantic relationships should be a joint adventure, where intolerance has no place to venture.

Intolerance causes arguments, stress, frustration and discontent.

Whilst patience, on the other hand, gives us time to think and understand.

Time to question our point of view, time to determine what to say or do.

R for Relationships

Intolerance has no moral dimension; its views will always be in contention.

So, when you engage in a romantic adventure let consideration for each other be at the centre.

Disregard any selfish intensions if you want your relationships to be successful.

Tolerance however **should never mean passivity** or **resignation to another person's control or influence**; and this is equally important in dating relationships.

Dating relationships?

Internet dating, probably the most common meeting strategy these days, pairs you up with someone you have never met before.

It's not like **getting to know someone over a period of time** at college, university or work, for example. It's not surprising, therefore, that a high percentage of internet dates, **do not** end up in long-term commitments.

So, what's going on, do you think?

Well, before trying to answer that question, which we probably won't be able to anyway, let's read another poem entitled, **Disillusioned Dater**.

Disillusioned Dater

Let's give it a go, one more time, maybe this is the one I can claim as mine.

Let's talk REACH

Oh no… have I got it wrong? Don't think I'll be staying here for long.

First impressions: not too keen, but I'll stick it out, mustn't appear too mean.

A quick hello and then I'll be off… but just a minute, maybe not.

I'm feeling something I never felt before. Oh gosh, I nearly walked out of the door.

Talked and found some common ground, minds entwined in sights and sound.

New emotions, feeling secure, new horizons and wanting more.

Have I met the one at last, with whom I can share my life and discard the past?

Is this actually what it seems, or am I simply having a dream? Well, at least I'm going to give it a try. It's all too easy to say goodbye.

The disillusioned dater above, was probably (initially) put off by the other's **appearance**. After all, that's all they had to go on, apart from, maybe a phone call or two, and appearance is a strong motivating factor; we do need to feel some degree of physical attraction.

Interestingly, however, how often have you looked at a couple in a pub or restaurant and thought to yourself, **what do those two see in one another?**

Often.

The old saying, 'beauty is only skin deep', is probably applicable in a situation like this. But, back to the poem.

R for Relationships

The disillusioned dater was hoping to experience something a bit special this time, having probably been on too many dates to remember, only to have been disappointed.

And at first, the individual was put off, but then the atmosphere changed. Something was said, or an expression revealed something special, something that sparked an interest that they may never have experienced in quite the same way before. **The 'chemistry' was different this time.**

I know you are probably thinking. Oh, you were...

Yes, I've had the same kind of experiences myself. It felt great at the time, and it was exiting, but it didn't last.

I'm sorry to hear that – but it can happen, obviously. Probably, you discovered that you had some interests in common, some of the same desires and expectations, and you were even beginning to 'fancy' the other person physically. But there were other things you were not quite sure about.

Just remember, as the first line of the poem, **Relationships**, states:

Relationships have a purpose, that's why, of course, they exist.

Well, yes – that's obvious.

And whilst in life we engage in many kinds of relationships, including family, friendships, work colleagues, and so on, and they all have their own specific **purposes** and **requirements**, romantic relationship are far more complex.

Some of the **hoped-for requirements** and the **responsibility requirements** are expressed in the following poem, entitled, **Romantic Ties**.

Let's talk REACH

Romantic Ties

Lives entwined with mutual respect, wanting for your partner what you would expect.

Times of great joy, and sometimes displeasure, but these are events that need to be worked through together.

Giving and sharing, hoping and daring, treasures and pleasures and support when despairing.

Loving and caring without critical comparing, whilst revealing one's feelings without being overbearing.

Commitment through trials, restricting self-pleasure, that threatens the union of one's lifelong treasure.

Behaviours controlled by thoughts for each other, for example, being aware of the stress of a new mother.

To share the chores that life hands out, with no complaints about what it's about.

Responsibilities shared, when all you want is rest, but these are the times when we must rise to the test.

Anxiety, worry, ill-health or whatever, the things that you may have to deal with together.

Commitment despite what might seem easier elsewhere, but make no mistake, the answer may not be out there.

I don't know whether you are in a romantic relationship at the moment, in the early stages of a romantic relationship, or in a long-established romantic relationship, but what I can be sure of is this.

R for Relationships

You, because of forethought and experience, could add any number of other important messages to the above poem, because you are an individual, with your own 'particular outlook on life'.

And with the above in mind, it might be worth pointing out the following:

Being naturally beautiful or handsome is something over which we have little control. Those characteristics **might** give you some advantages in life, **but not necessarily**.

Being healthy in body and mind however, is something over which most of us **do have some control** – and those characteristics, in the long-term, are more precious, more valuable and more beneficial than any outward features.

It's a shame that the media, magazines, the internet etc. doesn't portray this sentiment. More often there are just too many pressures, particularly on women, to have a particular look.

You are right, but I think that some things are beginning to change. It just needs more people, like you, to speak out about it.

In this context, I once heard it said that **inner beauty** was **far more beneficial than any outward features**. As we age, our appearance will change; we will look older (obviously) and, chances are, will not be as 'attractive' as we once were. **Inner beauty**, however, reflected in those characteristics which make an individual **'desirable to be with'**, can improve with age. If we can recognise any 'deficiencies' and modify our behaviour (if needs be).

Even so, whilst physical attraction may become less important as we get older, there's no excuse for slovenly dress or a dishevelled appearance, which can obviously detract from anyone's appeal.

Let's talk REACH

And for those who, for whatever reasons, don't feel particularly confident about their looks or appearance, there's nothing wrong with making a few changes appearance-wise; cloths, make-up (if appropriate), you know what I mean. After all, the way a person looks says a lot about the kind of person they are.

Now, whilst the characteristics that make one individual 'desirable' to another can be very different, and for lots of different reasons (obviously), I think it's fair to say that **patience** and **tolerance** would be fairly high on anyone's list.

I agree. But sometimes you can get so irritated or annoyed by someone else's behaviour, that losing your patience is unavoidable.

That's understandable, I can't deny, but extremes of impatience, as the following poem illustrates, is far from ideal.

Impatient; That's Me.

An impatient mind is like a coiled-up spring; no restraint, no way to keep my frustration in.

Why, because to tolerate the whims of others, is not something with which I wished to be bothered.

So, I say, what's your game? Sort yourself out, don't let your issues mess me about.

When I need to rush, that's what I do, and it doesn't need to be of any concern to you.

Providing you don't get in my way or hinder my path, we'll get on fine, it's as simple as that.

R for Relationships

Yes, a bit over the top, I think. The person speaking in this poem might need to do some self-analysis.

And in the context of self-analysis, you might like to ask yourself this question:

Is impatience, in any situation, likely to be beneficial in any way, or could it even, possibly, have negative health implications?

Well, to experience the emotional feelings related to impatience, may not be good for us health-wise, but the result of impatience, it has to be acknowledged can, in some situations, be beneficial.

For example, there are in life, certain jobs or professions where a quick decision can be extremely important. There may not be time to consider all the options; delays can put lives at risk or lead to serious consequences. Paramedics and the police, for example, may have to make quick decision, in all sorts of situations.

OK, point taken, and whilst the following poem doesn't relate to the kind of **quick decisions** that you have just mentioned, it does make reference to those everyday 'ordinary decisions' that people might need to make quickly, that could be beneficial. It's entitled, **Patience, or What?**

Patience, or What?

Patience to some might seem absurd, because in some situations it's best not observed.

Waiting too long can leave you deprived, and you can miss opportunities where you could really have thrived.

So, patience is fine, if its timely and planned, and results in conclusions which play into your hands.

Let's talk REACH

Waiting and watching, considering and informing, are the best ways to ensure that patience is rewarding.

It's just a matter of the right situation, and taking all into account, with due consideration.

With this approach, and a happy disposition, you should ensure that your life reflects a contented condition.

The above poem does (we have to acknowledge) highlight some fair points related to the 'benefits' of impatience, but the following poem makes some counter arguments. It's entitled, **Impatience Demands**.

Impatience Demands

Impatience can demand that we act right away, to avoid the consequences of any kind of delay.

But impatience robs us of 'thinking time', which should be taking place in a thoughtful mind.

Because whilst rushed decisions may go to plan, in hindsight we often realise that we had, in fact, got it wrong.

But how to avoid this dilemma, when impatience is such a powerful compeller?

Maybe our impulses need addressing, the ones that the mind finds so distressing.

Just a minute. We have just read and discussed three poems that express different points of view related to patience or impatience. Clearly things in this context are not necessarily clear cut.

R for Relationships

That's true. For example, reflexes (which are uncontrolled rapid reactions) can be very beneficial in protecting us from harm or injury.

And as you pointed out, some responses are so urgent that **delays**, in some situations, could result in serious consequences.

However, actions that are **not quite as urgent**, would often benefit from more thought, care and attention. By allowing ourselves more **thinking time**, we are less likely **to make mistakes**, which could affect others, as well as ourselves.

A few examples of the above are suggested below:

- Displays of anger, **which are not justified.**
- Losing your temper, **without knowing all the facts.**
- Aggressive driving **which benefits no one.**
- Shouting at our friend, a partner or the children, **when we are tired.**

Patience, gives us the opportunity **to think**, **reflect** and **evaluate**, before we 'communicate', react or behave which has the potential to result in a better outcome for ourselves, as well as others, in the kind of situations listed above. And the reason is: **we are social animals**, and 'getting on with one another' goes some way towards creating a better society in which we all live.

But getting on with people is related to all sorts of factors, not just patience!

I agree, but I think you might be quite surprised at just how 'influential' patience can be, related to all sorts of factors.

Whilst impatience often results in behaviour characterised by hasty or impromptu actions (often aimed at personal satisfaction), patient behaviour is much more 'considered'.

Let's talk REACH

Patience, **the investment of time and effort** into making decisions or taking actions to achieve a desired result, allows for **a re-education of the thought processes**.

A re-education of the thought processes!

Yes. Patience is not the magic bullet in this process, but it is a 'vehicle' **which provides an opportunity** for this to take place.

As mentioned before, **the subconscious mind** has access to our memories, experiences, images, emotions, and so on (stored unconsciously over the years) and can use these **to influence our conscious thinking** and **subsequent behaviour**. We need to remain aware of this, and maybe take time to consider how our current thinking **might** have been affected by this 'stored information'. And if it has, maybe consider if we need to do some things differently.

It's clear, from all that we have discussed so far, that **just being us**, with all the complications that this can create, can make life quite difficult to navigate, to say the least.

Consider now, however, how much more difficult, unpleasant, threatening and even frightening life can become when the more unpleasant individuals amongst us involve themselves in our lives. I refer to the **bullies**, the **racists**, the **sexists** and the **domestic abusers**. As distressing as these issues are, we do need to give them our attention.

So, let's do this now, and start with **bullying**.

Bullying has happened throughout history, and today **people in all age groups**, from primary school children through to adults in old age, may experience bullying. The ABA (Anti-Bullying Alliance) define bullying as follows:

R for Relationships

The repetitive, intentional hurting of one person or group by another person or group, where the relationship involves an imbalance of power.

Bullying has many forms. It can take place on our **streets**, in our **schools, colleges, universities, workplaces, care homes**, and even in the **family home**. And of course, it takes place **on online** and **over the phone**.

Bullying can be hugely distressing, and the mind begins to be tormented **with thoughts of self-criticism**. Stress and anxiety cloud the judgment and questions such as '**what's wrong with me?**' begin to be asked. **But it's not the victim who is at fault – it's the bully who has the issue.**

Read the following poem, **It's What I Am**, to reveal some important truths.

The first part highlights the distressing thoughts of the individual represented in this poem, and the second half addresses some of their thinking and, in conclusion, warns the bully of the risks to their own mental health, that can result from their behaviour.

It's What I Am

So what if I'm a bully? What concern is that of yours? I seek my pleasure where I can, by tormenting people's minds. I love to see my victims suffer; it makes me laugh out loud, of what I say and who I hurt; I truly do feel proud.

Some say I got it from my dad, or maybe I'm just jealous. Some say I'm simply prejudiced, and only like to menace. It may be their appearance, disabilities or special needs, it makes no odds to me, it's the satisfaction on which I feed.

Let's talk REACH

So now you understand me; this is what I am. I'm fine, no need to fuss or try to change my plan.

I'm sorry, but I can't leave it there, you need to turn your life around. Bullies are not born that way; it's life that's dragged you down. Maybe it's insecurity that feeds your troubled mind, or anger, or frustration, or things you've been denied.

But what you need to know, because it is so true, just as you damage other lives, your life is damaged too. Bullies find it hard you see when emotions are concerned, to form close relationships, and that's really no surprise.

So, with this in mind, you might decide to change how you behave. There's nothing clever, nothing to be gained from your evil ways.

Whilst the individual in this poem **might have been at school** at the time and engaged in 'typical' bullying tactics, bullying can involve much more 'subtle' behaviour, and can take place in any location.

Anyone who is being bullied **at university or college** should speak to someone in their **Student Union** for help and advice. In fact, if you are struggling with any issues, exam pressure, or mental health issues related to any cause, don't delay in arranging a meeting with a Student Union representative, and you can always talk to your course tutor.

Bullying in the workplace can involve many different forms of intimidation. The **misuse of power is common**, and can sometime be **cumulative**, where the bully, through a series of smaller attacks, carries out **a campaign of bullying** against their victim for many different reasons. In addition, an individual can be targeted simply because they are 'different' in some way, and unwanted physical contact, or offensive language, all count as bullying.

R for Relationships

Bullying in the workplace should never be left unchallenged. Any employment contract should include 'wording' stating that the employer will provide reasonable support to protect their staff from bullying and unwanted harassment from colleagues.

Seeking support and help from a trusted friend is always advisable when challenging intimidating behaviour at work, and the internet can provide all the information needed to challenge bullying behaviour in a safe and effective way. And **a Union representative** will often be available **to provide help and support too**.

You may have a family member in a **residential home, care home,** or **similar environment**, and if you believe that they are being bullied in any way, seek appropriate help straight away. No one has the right to bully another, and no one should feel distressed or threatened by the actions of a bully.

Bullying very often starts at school, and there are a multitude of reasons why bullying takes place. However, whilst the victims of bullying might blame themselves, suggesting that they are being bullied because of some 'negative characteristic' of their own, this perception must be challenged by teachers, peers and parents.

It's the bully who has the issues, not the victim. A bully may not know why they behave this way. Maybe it's insecurity, anger or frustration that drives their behaviour. But for sure, **one of the motivations is power**. Bullies like to feel powerful and make their victims feel weak; but we need to prove them wrong. Sometimes this can require the help of a friend, and this is illustrated in the following poem entitled, **Feelings**.

Feelings

Don't feel like saying anything anymore. They've said it all, I know the score.

Let's talk REACH

No! Don't get down – their words are groundless and as you know their thoughts are mindless.

So how do I deal with this appalling feeling and words that have no truthful meaning?

Ignore them, deny them the pain they're seeking; they don't deserve a moment's hearing.

But what about the way I'm feeling: degraded, insignificant, no chance of healing.

Is this you that they're describing? No – it's their distorted minds unwinding.

In short, your advice is to ignore them; turn my back and disregard them?

Yes. Together we will disarm them, and soon enough, we will discard them.

But behind a screen the bullies hide, with powerful technologies on their side.

True, and having a place to hide, and with nothing but torment on their mind.

So, will you help me to survive, to rebuild my confidence and again feel alive?

I will, and let's deny them the shameful deeds which they rely on.

Where we can, and if we can, whilst keeping ourselves safe, we should help our friends (and others) to become free of the bully's despicable behaviour.

R for Relationships

And can I say something?

Of course.

Anyone who is being bullied, in any situation, can contact the National Bullying Helpline. They can be emailed at help@nationalbullyinghelpline.co.uk *or contacted by phone on 0300 323 0169.*

Thank you for that information.

OK, let's move on. Another hugely distressing behaviour is **racism**.

Racism, characterised by **the display of prejudice, discrimination, or antagonism** against a person or group based on their membership of a particular racial or ethnic group, is another distressing behaviour which deserves some serious discussion.

But, for a non-expert (like myself), to talk with any degree of authority on the causes of racisms, or the consequences of racism on the individual or society in general, is, well, unrealistic. **And** for an ordinary (non-expert) member of the public to similarly engage, is probably equally unrealistic.

So, what are we supposed to do, ignore the problem and carry on behaving either 'pleasantly' or 'unpleasantly' towards our fellow human beings, as we have always done?

Pleasantly, yes – but unpleasantly, not in my opinion. So maybe, if nothing else, we could consider some of the psychological theories related to racism that might dissuade any racists, or potential racist (that might be reading this book), to reconsider their behaviour. But first, let's read another poem. It's entitled, **I'm a Racist**.

Let's talk REACH

I'm a Racist

I heard you chanting on the terraces, it was not a pleasant sound. In fact, it was quite disgraceful, but I expect you feel quite proud?

I do indeed, absolutely. I'm a racist through and through. I don't give a jot about what you think, because it's what I choose to do.

Tell me though, why you do it, what's the motivation? What do you gain, what do you feel, what's your inspiration?

I feel a sense of purpose, to show them who I am; a white man, a proud man, in a white man's land.

So, if you needed a dentist, a doctor or a nurse, you'd disregard their services if their skin was dark, and ask for someone else?

No, not exactly – that's not what I would do, because I realise that they are here, and this is what they do.

You're on really shaky ground right now; I can't believe what you've just said. Is this actually you whose talking, or another's influence instead?

I used to think I knew you, in fact, I'm sure I did, but you've changed, you're different, someone's clearly got inside you head.

I know I'm not the one I used to be, and maybe I don't feel proud, but give me time, and with some help, I might be able to turn my life around.

The racist speaking in this poem, at first displays no regret regarding their behaviour, and in fact appears to be quite proud of their activities and clearly has no compassion.

R for Relationships

Do you know anyone who behaves like this? As the poem asks:

Tell me though, why you do it, what's the motivation? What do you gain, what do you feel, what's your inspiration?

Later, the racist is asked to think about their attitudes when confronted with the question related to being treated by someone in the medical profession who has a different skin colour to their own.

Later still, they appear, maybe, to be having second thoughts about their attitudes and behaviour, especially since they admit that:

I know I'm not the one I used to be, and maybe I don't feel proud, but give me time, and with some help, I might be able to turn my life around.

With the above in mind, let's give some thought to some of the theories related to racism, its potential causes and its possible consequences.

One of the psychological theories of racism suggests that the perpetrator (the racist) fears that **their own security is being threatened** in some way, or that **their own importance is at stake**, or that **they are at risk of losing control**. This suggests a lot of insecurity on the part of the racist.

Yes, I agree with this.

Another theory suggests that a racist might have a deep seated, and probably unconscious feeling **that they are not good enough** (have a low opinion of themselves).

Yes, that's possible.

The need to belong is a basic human requirement and **a powerful motivating force**. It could be suggested that some individuals who lack a sense of security may be attracted to groups that gives them an identity and a common cause.

Let's talk REACH

That may be the case, but any behaviour directed by an individual or group towards others that causes harm or distress does no justice to the role of responsible, compassionate or beneficial human activity.

I agree completely. Racism is hugely destructive, and the everyday experiences of many individuals in our society demonstrate this. Not only can it drastically affect **the victims mental** and **physical well-being**, but it can also have **a devastating effect** on **local community life** and **society in general**.

So **why** do so many people behave in this way?

Some of the above theories may be correct, but it's not an easy question to answer.

I agree. But whatever factors or motivation results in one human being racially abusing another, **there is something that the racist needs to be aware of**, and maybe it needs to be **talked about** more widely.

And that is?

The following fact. Not only can the racist's behaviour **damage other people's lives**, but their behaviour **can damage their own lives** too. The long-term effects upon the racist can include: torment, regret, shame and so much more, and the damage to their own mental health can have life-changing consequences.

So, are you suggesting that this is a message that racist individuals need to be aware of?

I think so, because life would be so much better for everyone, if respect, trust and security existed in all aspects of our lives. Would you agree?

R for Relationships

Absolutely.

Whilst the above reflects a lot of disturbing elements relating to racism, things are beginning to change. Men and women of different colour are frequently seen together these days (which is fantastic) and often with their grown-up children. Furthermore, children in many of our schools play with others of mixed ethnicity and accept the situation as 'normal'.

The following poem is an interesting reflection of the perceptions of racism in an unusual situation. It's entitled, **Darkness Revealed**.

Darkness Revealed

The lights went out, I tripped and stumbled, the lightning flashed, and the thunder rumbled.

Don't mess about, put the lights back on. It wasn't me (said a voice), it's what the lightning's done.

Confusion reigned for a very long time, but then a helping hand at last found mine.

He helped me up. Well, I assumed it was a 'he'; whoever it was, it was a relief to me.

When the lights came on, and to my surprise, there was a young black man standing by my side.

For a moment, my thoughts were in confusion; he was black, I was white, was this an illusion?

I've never considered myself to be a racist, but my boyfriends had always been Caucasian.

Let's talk REACH

But the events of that night were a revelation; how could colour create such discrimination?

We talked and laughed and planned our next meeting. It seems ages since that eventful evening.

We've been together now for six months or more. He's lovely, gentle and generous to the core.

But a friend of mine asked recently. When the lights came on, what did you see?

I saw a human being, just like me, and his colour faded into tranquillity.

Before, I was probably just colour-blind. I see differently now; I've had a change of mind.

A very moving and thought-provoking poem.

We don't know (because the poem doesn't tell us) where this event took place. Probably, it was a night club or similar venue. But what we do know, is that a young woman (because of her experience one evening, during a thunderstorm) came to realise that probably she had previously (in her own words) been colour-blind.

Whilst physical attraction is hugely important at the beginning of a romantic relationship, **the process of getting to know someone** can be complex.

The reasons why the man and woman (in the poem) felt such a strong attraction to one another could only be answered by themselves.

But let's be clear, **the initial getting to know someone** and the potential **getting on with someone**, will be influenced by **many**

R for Relationships

different **personal characteristics**, and in terms of **romantic relationships**, you would probably agree that the following, are pretty important:

Caring – gentle – compassionate – reliable – considerate – honest.

And **respect**, **trust** and **security** (mentioned previously) should, obviously, be added to the list.

Whilst the contents of the poem, **Darkness Revealed**, provided (even if only momentarily) a glimmer of hope that one day racism might not exist, for the victims of racism (today), **respect, trust or security**, does **not** exist.

Neither, unfortunately, does **respect, trust or security** exist in **the everyday experiences of many women and girls** across our land **who experience sexism**. So, let's give this hugely important and distressing topic some thought now.

Sexism

Sexism is the oppression, abuse and mistreatment of women and girls by dominant males, **sometimes** based on the belief **that one sex is intrinsically superior to another**. At its extreme, sexism includes sexual abuse, harassment, rape and other forms of sexual violence.

Harassment, intimidation, aggression, physical or sexual violence perpetrated by a man or boy towards a women or girl, is an abhorrent act. What is wrong with some males?

Not the easiest question to answer.

Fear of such behaviour causes **anxiety** and **destress** to tens of thousands of women and girls on a daily basis in our schools, on our streets, in clubs, universities, workplaces and even in the home. **Beyond the fear**, an actual physical act can result in physical injury, mental trauma and in extreme cases, it can tragically result in death.

So how do we begin to address this very disturbing issue? The following poem, **The Great Revealing**, sets the scene and makes some suggestions.

The Great Revealing

When we were children, four or five, we were innocent in both body and mind. Mischievous, yes, naughty too, but with nothing physical of which we knew.

But soon enough, as time went by, with body changes and new awareness, puberty revealed our gender differences, which led to blushes and often shyness.

Sounds and sights, new joys revealing, with innocence no more concealing, and responsibility taking on new meaning, not only for ourselves, but for other's feelings.

But this is when immaturity can threaten, and where disrespect over decency beckons. When men and boys can lose compassion, and their hidden demons begin to threaten.

But with increasing age and adult thinking, one would hope to see respect revealing, with maturity being the key to unlock a sense of responsibility.

Verse four makes reference to immaturity, and how disrespect over decency beckons. And the last verse suggests that ...with increasing age and adult thinking, one would hope to see respect revealing, with maturity being the key, to unlock a sense of responsibility.

R for Relationships

In the experience of the young women **speaking in the next poem**, however, **respect shows no sign of revealing**, related to the young man to whom she is speaking.

And she doesn't hold back about her feelings as she raises some very valid and important issues in the poem, **Sexism Experienced**.

Sexism Experienced

Get your dirty hands off me and turn your life around. What makes you think you have the right to violate and hound?

What's eating at your mind, what thoughts do you compare, to decent men and boys, just take your hands elsewhere.

You say some quite disgraceful things, are you not aware of how your words offend and hurt and even cause great fear?

Your acts are really shameful. How did they first arise; were they nurtured in the home, and to you no real surprise?

Or is it how your peers behave that have triggered your demise? And are you influenced to behave against your true desires?

You may be physically bigger than me, and even feel superior, but get it in your mind, young man, you really are inferior.

Do you think it's how things are; the case of social norms. Are you supposed to think this way because you were born a boy?

Or maybe it's just gender roles, the way things used to be. No, times have changed, I'll make it clear, you really need to see.

Your thoughts, your tone, your actions, we clearly don't accept. There's nothing macho, nothing brave, and nothing worthy of respect.

Let's talk REACH

Of course, we're sexually different, the reasons are quite clear: our biological purposes are to reproduce and share.

But let's remember that the female gender has qualities males have not. You may not, of course, be aware of this, because you've probably lost the plot.

But if allowed to flourish and without discrimination, our shared lives have the potential, to make life so rich and special.

Well said, brilliant. She certainly doesn't hold back on her feelings!

And rightly so.

To answer the question, 'Why do some men and boys behave so appallingly towards women and girls?' is hugely complex and would require different experts from different disciplines to provide answers.

At this point, however, we do need to acknowledge that not only do women and girls get sexually abused by men or boys, but sexual abuse occurs within, and between members of any gender.

Very depressing!

So, to anyone who is ever likely to exhibit sexist behaviour towards anyone else, **consider this**:

Imagine for a moment **that Earth was invaded by an alien species** who, not only deplore sexual abuse in any form, but also have the technology (the know-how) to identify all human beings that engaged in these acts.

Furthermore, not only do they have the ability to identify these individuals, but the ability to expose them through the media, newspapers, TV, internet, and so on. And this was their aim.

R for Relationships

A terrifying thought to anyone who does or might consider carrying out such behaviour.

My hope is that any sexual abuser out there (who is reading this book) would reflect on what is being expressed above, read the poem again, and consider seriously their behaviour. Then decide how they might begin to **change their behaviour**, either **with the help of therapy**, or **as a result of self-will** and **determination**.

We ALL have a role to play in bringing this despicable behaviour to an end. Anyone who is out and about with someone who begins to display sexism in any form needs to speak out, show their disapproval. Anyone who chooses to ignore this behaviour in their presence is equally guilty, in my opinion.

Well said, you are absolutely right.

And here's another hugely distressing issue, which we should all be aware of and be prepared to talk about: **domestic abuse**.

There is no simple definition of domestic abuse, but it can be broadly defined as any incident or pattern of incidents of **controlling, coercive or threatening behaviour, violence or abuse between those aged sixteen or over who are or have been intimate partners or family members, regardless of gender or sexuality**.

Domestic abuse can include, but is not limited to:

- Controlling or coercive behaviour.
- Physical or sexual abuse.
- Violent or threatening behaviour.
- Economic abuse.
- Psychological and/or emotional abuse.

Let's talk REACH

Once again, for anyone reading this book who **feels threatened or intimidated in any way**, please seek **professional help** without delay. If you believe or feel that you are in immediate danger, call the police on 999. Alternatively, to access specialist domestic abuse support call Victim Support on 0808 168-9111.

Whilst women are the most likely victims of domestic abuse, and the abusers are usually men, men may also be abused, as well as children and elderly adult family members.

The woman speaking in the poem below is experiencing abuse in the family home. She feels desperate, and in her mind is trying to work out how to proceed; she is having **silent thoughts**.

Silent Thoughts

Turn around and walk away, no more your words or actions to dismay. You've made our lives too distressing to bear, no more your presence to despair.

Or else I'll have to walk away, but I know I'll need a place to stay. A place of refuge far away, where the kids and I can safely play.

It'll be over then, a time to settle, and let his demons be forgotten.

I'll plan it all with those I trust, we'll keep it quiet, we really must. Some things we'll have to leave behind, but that's a cost I do not mind.

We'll start again, the kids and I, and hope someday a prince we'll find; a person with a heart of gold, they're out there somewhere, so I've been told.

Someone to share our lives and treasure a family scene full of happiness and pleasure.

R for Relationships

Hopefully, the situation described above, **will never be in your experience**, but may well **be in your awareness**. If you become aware of any situation of domestic abuse, do what you can to help the victim **if they feel comfortable with your involvement**, and if you can proceed without putting yourself, or them, at risk.

Being abused physically or emotionally, including bullying, racism, sexism or domestic abuse, is distressing enough for an able-bodied person, but for **a disabled person**, the experience is likely to be even more traumatising, since being unable **to defend oneself** can, in many situations, become very serious, even life threatening.

With the above in mind, reflect on the following poem entitled, **My Disabilities**.

My Disabilities

In mind and body our disabilities to bear, you would think that our suffering would at least end there.

But no, some people choose to abuse us: partners, carers, family members and our disabilities can leave us defenceless.

Afraid to comment or show displeasure, we fear our complaints will attract 'whatever'.

Fourteen million people disabled; you would think we would have a voice at the table.

But if we don't which we often suspect, will you help us please to avoid this neglect.

To fight for our corner so that our lives can reflect, dignity, compassion love and respect.

Let's talk REACH

Abuse of any kind is disgraceful, but to suffer abuse as a disabled person makes the perpetrator (the abuser) seem inhumane. To target someone who not only has a disability, but often the inability to defend or protect themselves, is shocking.

I agree, completely, but before leaving this topic of abuse, which has included bullying, racisms, sexism, and domestic intimidation, it is important to be aware that abuse occurs in many other forms which are not necessarily at first apparent.

Type into any internet search engine, 'Types of abuse', and in addition to those already discussed, you will probably be shocked and surprised at how many different human activities fall into this category.

The next poem, which contains the reflections of **a wheelchair-bound individual**, expresses, **in a very unusual way**, thoughts related to being **scammed** by a **fraudster**. It's entitled, **Disability Uncovered**.

Disability Uncovered

Yes, I am disabled. More vulnerable than most to life's demanding challenges that can sometimes pip you at the post.

But you may not be aware of the benefits I've derived: resilience, determination and, when allowed, a chance to thrive.

We all have disabilities and yours you can often hide, but for me they're always on display to other's peering eyes.

But I seek the same enjoyments as you, the same surprises too. I only ask for appropriate facilities to help me to get through.

Just try to get your mind around the way I have to function, the way I have to plan my time to avoid delays and survive disruption.

R for Relationships

But that's enough about me for now, it's time for your surprise. I'm going to tell you something now that might open up your eyes.

You may think you're not disabled; you may think that you're all right, but just read the definition below, it just might change your mind.

A person has a disability if they are physically or mentally impaired and if this has a long-term adverse effect upon their ability to function; to carry out the normal day-to-day activities to which they wish to be accustomed.

Part of the normal day-to-day activities of a decent human being, should be to treat others as they would expect to be treated, if you get my meaning.

But if, for example, you live your life as a fraudster by design, then don't be surprised to be labelled disabled, because that's what's on my mind.

It may not be a diagnosed condition, but if it applies to you, if you're not happy with the term disability, will the term disgraceful do?

More thought-provoking sentiments expressed above. Yes, there are some 'disgraceful' individuals at large in society.

Yes, including fraudsters and criminals of every kind who are prepared **to take what is not theirs**, and as a consequence **damage other people's lives or livelihoods**. For society to be a better place for everyone, we all need to behave responsibly, and with compassion towards others, including those we have never met.

But is everyone capable of this?

Clearly not, but as expressed in the poem, **First Thought**, and despite childhood experiences that **might** have negatively impacted on our behaviours:

Let's talk REACH

...you're not a robot, you're a human creation.

With a little effort and determination, you can make the right interpretations.

I'd like to think that fraudsters and criminals of every type, if they have a conscience, would reflect on their behaviours, and put their efforts into more wholesome pursuits, to the benefit of others. A naïve hope, maybe, but if **some** are prepared to change their behaviours, not only would their potential victims not be affected, but the potential impact on their own long-term mental health, could be avoided.

And for the rest of us 'ordinary members of the human race' who are not perfect (obviously) but try to live a 'decent sort of life', but still exhibit behaviours that affect others adversely, making a little effort and determination can go a long way too.

The problem is, although the human brain is (in essence) a supercomputer, and makes most decisions and reactions at lighting speed, **this can be a disadvantage**, especially when we are about to communicate, react or behave in some way. On some occasions, **pressing the pause button** can be really helpful to give us **time** to think before we act, because (as has been suggested previously) the way we feel can have such a powerful effect **on what happens next** (our responses).

So, by pausing briefly, we can:

1. Consider carefully **what has caused the feelings** that we are experiencing.
2. Consider logically, sensibly and appropriately, **what our responses should be**.

So, let's keep all of the above in mind as we move on and think about **E for Enjoyment.**

E for Enjoyment

Whilst **survival** is the **primary driving force** of **human activity**, **enjoyment**, the **positive emotional** and **physical responses** to our experiences, contributes hugely to that process.

However, whilst discussing enjoyment in this chapter, we must keep in mind that **enjoyment** usually implies **a short-term sensory experience**. Sustaining **a long-term positive emotional experience** and **physical state**, however, are some of the ingredients associated with **happiness**.

The problem is, life by its very nature is incredibly complex and enjoyment can be fleeting, and sometimes it can be scarce. Sometimes it is not appropriate due to suffering or bereavement, and sometimes circumstances beyond our control (such as the '20-'22 Covid pandemic) can have a huge impact on our capacity for enjoyment.

And as illustrated in the previous chapter, the behaviour of the 'not so pleasant' individuals amongst us can have a devastating impact on the happiness, well-being and enjoyment of others.

But let's not get too gloomy. Let's see if we can get our minds around some of the mechanics of enjoyment, and let's begin by reading the simple poem below entitled, **The Enjoyment Factor**.

The Enjoyment Factor

Enjoyment can be a state of mind created by a touch, a taste, a smell, a sight or sound.

And when striving for personal needs, enjoyment can be found in what we can achieve.

It can also be experienced through human interactions, giving, sharing and good intentions.

And let's not forget the role of mother nature's creations, their therapeutic features and joyous sensations.

Enjoyment is a basic human need, and upon its experience we all can feed.

So, when we can let's raise a smile and create for all a pleasant time, and let enjoyment be the test that we've all tried to do our best.

So, the poem is suggesting that enjoyment can be **a state of mind** resulting from: the information received via the senses, the result of our achievements, our interactions with other people, and our experiences of the natural world.

OK, but all of these 'situations' have their own individual levels of complexity.

Of course, **and some people** find enjoyment **so much more difficult to achieve**, that others.

So, you are now going to tell me WHY, some people appear to find enjoyment so much more difficult to achieve, that others.

Well, partly yes, but I'm no expert.

I accept that, but let's see what you have to say.

OK. Firstly, you have to bear in mind that other people may not be **as confident** as you are, or **as relaxed in company**, or **as self-assured**.

Then there is **financial insecurity**. Some people struggle more than others in this connection for a variety of reasons, and most people enjoy buying things that give them enjoyment.

E for Enjoyment

Ill health, misfortune, bereavement or **family problems** are other major issues that can impact on someone's enjoyment in life.

Not enjoying your work or study environment can raise all sorts of issues that can affect one's enjoyment too.

And obviously, **being abused** in various ways can impact on an individual's enjoyment in life enormously.

And then there's **personality**. I could suggest that personality could impact on one's enjoyment.

After all, personality can have an impact on one's ability to engage in successful relationships, and successful relationships tend to be enjoyable relationships.

So, in relation to what you have just said, being us (to use your expression) could be part of the problem.

Well, yes.

Anyone who has the tendency to be 'less that positive' about life in general, and certainly if they struggle within interpersonal relationships, then they might need to give some thought to the following.

People who make situations in life more enjoyable are usually:

Full of life .... not tiresome.
Generous .... not selfish.
Compassionate .... not hard-hearted.
Non-judgemental .... not critical.
Interesting to know .... not boring.
Open minded .... not having fixed ideas.
Caring .... not thoughtless.
Fun to be with .... not gloomy.
Cheerful .... not moody.

Let's talk REACH

And in this context, **self-awareness** and **emotional intelligence** (discussed previously) might be something to think about, if the 'whoever' wishes to be the kind of person that others are happy to associate with.

It's all very well expecting people to be full of life, generous, compassionate, non-judgemental, and so on, but LIFE, with all its worries, uncertainties and problems can take its toll on people. It's a big ask, to expect a lot of the above.

And sometimes you just don't feel brilliant yourself!

I know.

Sometimes things keep going wrong.

Like when you mess things up, or it takes too long.

Maybe you have too much to do.

And you don't have time to think things through.

And at the other extreme you have nothing to do.

Boring, tedious and depressing too.

Arguments leave you wondering, was it my fault?

Mind in torment, worry and doubt.

Not happy with the job at all.

Not much fun, can't take it anymore.

Money in short supply, what can I do?

Calm down, sit down, and think things through.

E for Enjoyment

Don't even feel particularly well.

Understandable, but chances are it's just a passing spell.

Do you realise that we have just written a poem together – and it raises some every day, matter-of-fact situations that could get anyone down.

Clearly, enjoyment is a complex issue. But for the purpose of keeping things fairly simple, let's keep in mind the above-mentioned statement that enjoyment is **a positive emotional and physical response** to our experiences.

But let's also keep in mind the fact that we don't all (obviously) experience **the same positive emotional and physical responses to the same things**. We are all different, and what one person might thoroughly enjoy, another might hate.

Absolutely. Some people enjoy high-risk sports, whilst others would find the experience terrifying.

Good example.

The bottom line is this (as I see it): experiences have the power to create enjoyment, or not and what we enjoy, or not, can be influenced by many factors. And in this context, I have just thought of something.

Oh, yes?

Imagine that you had never seen or tasted a **kiwi fruit**, but someone offered you one during your lunch break. Your first impressions might be: that's a strange-looking 'object' – can't imagine liking one of those. But you try it, and you love it. Why have I never tried one of these before, you are thinking.

Let's talk REACH

So, your point?

Well, my point is this. In life there are times when situations arise when we have the opportunity to try something new, do something different, take risks even, but, as the following poem points out, we often make:

Excuses

It's not surprising that enjoyable horizons at times elude our achieving. Because when opportunities arise that could satisfy our desires, we often find excuses not to pursue them.

It's so easy to say, 'that doesn't interest me', but how can you possibly know? Unless you've tried it before and it really was a bore, then why not give it a go?

Sometimes it's just insecurity, you'd feel a fool if 'whatever' went wrong. But don't let these frustrations prevent you from pursuing situations, which might never again come along?

Could it simply be lack of confidence, is it this which is holding you back? Just remember that confidence can be acquired by experience, and this must be part of your plan.

Is it rejection you fear, someone ignoring your heart-felt intentions? Don't let this get you down, don't let doubt taunt your mind, there'll always be new situations.

The above poem illustrates just a few of the endless possible excuses within different situations that if not challenged can result in us missing out on things in life, that could have provided enjoyment.

Often, it's just a matter of **overcoming your fears**, because that's what they are. Sometimes we have to **'face our fears'**. Easier said than done I know. **So, try this:**

E for Enjoyment

Make a decision to act. Think about **'what could go wrong'** and how you could deal with the **going wrong bit** if it happened, **then do it!**

OK, this is an interesting suggestion – a possible way forward, worth thinking about, yes.

I know that enjoying ourselves can sound complicated, but **effort – our own** or **someone else's**, tends to be **the catalyst** that **triggers enjoyment**.

Everyone (I think) enjoys watching a **good** film or TV program, and these result from other people's efforts.

But 'good' to one person, might be awful to another.

True.

So, ideally, **putting in an effort yourself** and directing it towards something **you think you are likely to enjoy** is likely to produce the best results. That's why people:

- Pursue creative activities related to specific interests or skills.
- Read books of their own choosing.
- Listen to music that they know they will enjoy.
- Socialise with people with whom they feel at ease.
- Exercise because it can lift the mood and enhance their health.
- Study for the joy of learning or for the prospect of rewards in the future.
- Stimulate the senses by experiencing the bountiful treasures of the natural world.

But a person may gain enjoyment by putting in an effort for someone else's benefit. It doesn't have to be a selfish thing.

I agree, and providing enjoyment emanates from wholesome intentions; it has the power to make those **less enjoyable issues** in our own lives, **a little easier to deal with** (most of the time).

And, **at the best of times**, enjoyment has the power **to generate energy** that spills over into other aspects of our lives, and other people's lives too.

OK, let's recap. Enjoyment can be fleeting, and sometimes it can be scarce (for all sorts of reasons) and lack of enjoyment can be our own fault, yes?

Well, fault, might not be the best term, but it's difficult to deny **that it could be about us**. For most people, enjoyment is 'at its best' when they are sharing their experiences with others. Socialising with friends is a great way to 'let your hair down', have fun and meet new people, **but it's not for everyone**.

We have to recognise that there are lots of reasons why some people struggle to socialise in group situations. Let's consider just two:

Some people simply **lack confidence**. They may feel that they have nothing to say, nothing to contribute.

Others may prefer to remain **emotionally detached** because being emotionally detached helps protect them from the anxiety and stress that social interactions might provoke.

Whilst being perfectly understandable, both of the above scenarios can impact negatively on an individual's future happiness. In addition to restricting, one's social life, lack of self-confidence and social isolation can impact on:

- An individual's relationship with a partner (or future partner).
- One's career prospects.
- One's mental health.

E for Enjoyment

Overcoming lack of self-confidence is not necessarily going to be easy. The problem is: most of the things we are recommended to do, such as:

- Avoid negative thoughts.
- Work on self-image.
- Be non-judgemental.
- Live for the moment.

And so on, can require a great deal of effort, or even the input from a therapist. But for now – how about **trying something different**? Spend some time **making use of your five incredible senses** (mentioned in the first line of the poem, The Enjoyment Factor).

We frequently hear, in the media, people talking about the therapeutic benefit of being out and about in the natural world.

And it's true. Not only that, but I read somewhere that, 'The human drive to protect nature starts with noticing it and caring about it'.

Absolutely, and when out in the natural world we can **look** at beautiful flowers in bloom, trees with their infinite variety of shapes and forms, **listen** to bird song, animal calls, and the sound of a bubbling stream. We can pick up a pinecone or a fallen leaf and **feel** its texture and study the complexity of its design. We can **taste** wild blackberries or take them home to make a crumble or pie, and we can **smell** the wild flowers and the clean, fresh air. In other words, **we can show an interest in things we may not have given much thought to in the past**, and this, as you suggest, can also be the beginning of the 'caring process' for the natural world.

The following very simple poem illustrates how just **taking an interest** can, in unexpected ways, open up new possibilities. It's entitled, **The Duck**.

Let's talk REACH

The Duck

It was one of those mornings: frost on the ground, leaves underfoot making a crunching sound.

I walked through the park, just for a change, and stopped to watch a duck on the frozen lake.

I'd arranged to meet a friend at half past eight, but the excursion made me very late.

Sorry, Tom, have I held you up? I got delayed in the park, just watching a duck.

Was it a hen or was it a drake? They're very different, you can't make a mistake.

I don't know, I've never given it much thought, tell me about it as we walk.

The hen is the female, she's quite drab. The drake, well he's a colourful chap.

How do you know so much about ducks, is it something you've read about in one of your books?

No – I'm a member of the wildlife trust; join us next time, you really must.

Is it all blokes, or are there any girls?

Girls, absolutely, it's a really great bunch – and afterwards we go somewhere to talk and have lunch.

You could imagine this conversation continuing, and how going to the next wildlife trust meeting began the development a different

E for Enjoyment

kind of friendship, not only with Tom, but other members of the group too.

And **the desire to be interested** (I once heard it said), was the catalyst that propelled many people to be successful in life, and success often results in enjoyment and happiness.

I know that **the topic of ducks** might **fall on deaf ears** to others who may not have the slightest interest in ducks, but you never know, and if nothing else, chances are it will cause a laugh.

But don't just concentrate all of your interest in one particular area – this can make you **a rather boring individual**. Try to be interested in all things, well, not all, but lots of different things.

Why? Well, no, I didn't need to ask why. It's obvious.

It is (obvious) because the next time you are in a group situation, you will be less likely to feel uncomfortable because, chances are you will be able to **contribute your own thoughts and ideas to the proceeding**. As a result, you will **begin to gain confidence**, and **enjoy yourself more**.

And another thing, spend some time **observing other people**.

Observe **how confident people interact with others**. See if you can work out what they are doing or saying that makes their interactions so successful. Make it your aim to let other people's confidence inform you and teach you how to be more confident yourself.

Not least, try to become more **self-aware**: more aware of your own **positive attributes** and **capabilities**, but also those **irrational negative thoughts** which can often hinder your progress. And in this context, read the poem below which makes a few useful suggestions in this connection. It's entitled, **Tell Me**.

Let's talk REACH

Tell Me.

Tell me. Why are you so confident, what makes you so sure? How do you know that you can achieve your goals when others feel insecure?

Confidence is about 'believing' that you can tackle whatever's ahead, and not being fearful of failure, but taking risks, if needs be, instead.

The first thing to snare is the self-obsession affair, where doubt in the mind is the dominant kind. It's these thoughts that afflict you, control and restrict you, and these you must now leave behind.

So don't be afraid to take part and engage, a passive observer has little to gain. Let social interactions, and thoughtful distractions encourage you to take a more positive aim.

With this new incentive, and thoughts redirected, future challenges should present a wider perspective.

OK, this is just one person's suggestions concerning confidence, and I think that we are all aware that confidence can be affected by so many different factors. But having a belief in yourself and the conviction that you have the ability to meet life's challenges and not least a willingness to try, can have a powerful influence on one's enjoyment in life.

And what about enjoyment through creativity?

Creativity is the use of the imagination to originate ideas or create something new. It is responsible for many of the entertainments which we find so enjoyable in life: TV, cinema, theme parks, etc. and the numerous manufactured products which enhance our lives in so many different ways.

E for Enjoyment

Not least, other people's sporting abilities, creativity and skills can create an enormous sense of enjoyment when we watch a football game, cricket match, a tennis tournament, music event, and so on.

However, whilst the creativity of others is important to our enjoyment of life, **there's nothing quite as enjoyable** as that which we gain **as a result of our own creativity**.

Creativity activates the mind in incredible ways. It taps into our inner resources: our knowledge, insights, inspirations, passion and commitment. It feeds on the input of the five senses and motivates us through our imagination to achieve something special; something of our own creation.

Never underestimate the power of creativity for enjoyment, and don't let setbacks or impatience dampen your enthusiasm.

The following poem has something to say regarding **patience** in this context. It's entitled, **Patience Matters**.

Patience Matters.

In the pursuit of pleasure, through creativity or leisure, patience has a role to play, to help us to deliver.

Whilst considering the needs of others is an important consideration, for our own well-being we must also engage in pursuits that we enjoy doing.

To pursue with patience, creative tasks with skill and imagination can lift the spirit and engage the mind in hours of dedication.

And most important by developing patience in interests that give us pleasure, we can often create a work-life balance, which in times of stress should make us feel so much better.

Let's talk REACH

Whilst the anticipation of pursuing something enjoyable can result in **im**patience, which is understandable (particularly for children), experiencing **im**patience as an adult, **when it affects others**, is far from ideal.

The following short poem could have been written by someone who had experienced the impatient behaviour of a dangerous driver, or someone behaving inappropriately in a shop checkout queue, for example. It's entitled, **What Right?**

What Right?

What right do you have to be impatient; do you think you are a special case? Does self-importance make you different to other members of the human race?

Do the gains you make have a beneficial connotation, or does impatience sometimes lead you into unpleasant confrontations?

Does enjoyment always have to be at your own discretion, and does impatience have a part to play in gaining choice possessions?

If, for you, enjoyment is the dominant position, then maybe patience, rather than impatience, might be the way to gain its recognition.

This poem starts by asking: do we (actually) have a right to be impatient?

Surely the answer is yes, we do have that right, in some situations.

But, if expressing that right **affects others adversely**, then surely **that 'right' comes into question.**

E for Enjoyment

The following line from a verse in the poem, **REACH When All Is Said and Done** (which appears in my book, REACH for Teenagers) suggests that **respect** and **caring** should be the dominant position when **enjoyment** is in question. Selfishness and impatience, however, does not reflect these characteristics.

Enjoyment is ours to share, as long as we respect and care.

Anyway, we seem to have got off track a little. We were talking about the pursuit of **enjoyment** through **creative activities**. So, if you can, get involved:

Don't be afraid to have a go at home improvements, but don't do anything you are unsure about, which could put your health or safety at risk.

Gardening projects (if you have a garden or window box) can create hours of 'flowering enjoyment'.
Hobbies of every kind can be a great source of enjoyment for people of all ages.

You are right, enjoyment which we create ourselves through our own creativity is priceless. The rewards can be long lasting, unlike the sometimes-fleeting rewards that can come from other forms of enjoyment.

And nurturing **the desire to be interested** will, **if we need to**, broaden our horizons because no longer will we have nothing to talk about, nothing to contribute – in fact quite the opposite.

And for those who are **really not enjoying life very much at the moment**, the following poem provides a few encouragements. It's entitled, **It's OK**.

Let's talk REACH

It's OK

It's no surprise that life at times is hard and gets you down. And if this applies to you right now, it may be time to turn your life around.

Don't assume that you will always be low, don't just accept the situation. Get out-and-about, go with the flow, and raise your expectations.

Savour the beauties of a natural situation and let your senses experience a joyful elevation.

And when you feel able 'start a new conversation' but only if you feel comfortable and in a safe location.

Raise your spirits by discarding the anguish resulting from something you've failed to establish.

Don't let past experiences limit your possibilities. Open your eyes and seize new opportunities.

Look to the future with brave and realistic intentions and expand your mind into broader dimensions.

Wonder, amusement, laughter, excitement, it's yours to be had, search out your entitlement.

And with your new-found confidence, start enjoying the company of others and remember: *enjoyment is ours to share, as long as we respect and care.*

So, to conclude this chapter, lets read a poem that has a lot to say regarding respect and care, which is so important for ensuring and maintaining enjoyment within any kind of relationship. It's entitled, **Joint Attraction.**

E for Enjoyment

Joint Attraction

Relationships develop when there's a joint attraction, and enjoyment is experienced with mutual satisfaction.

A meeting of minds, of a friendly disposition, where concerns for each other's welfare is the dominant position.

Where empathy confirms reassurance and compassion, in times of distress and heartache, when understanding really matters.

Enjoyment is best assured when all concerned can play their part, whilst feeling valued and appreciated; that's enjoyment at the heart.

In expressing one's ideas no one should ever try to dominate the scene, because whilst we have our own opinion, others might quite simply not agree.

To cause a disagreement, by any form or means, does nothing for enjoyment; it's the opposite we need.

So, approach all situations with kindness on your mind, so enjoyment for everyone is never left behind.

There are a lot of thought-provoking issues raised in the above poem, including:

…mutual satisfaction, a friendly disposition, empathy, feeling valued and appreciated, not trying to dominate the scene, always having kindness on your mind.

And if we can practice the above, everyone has a better chance of enjoying their lives and their relationships.

So, is that it? Have we covered everything we need to be aware of; everything we need to do to ensure that life is as enjoyable as possible?

Let's talk REACH

I know you are joking, because of course we haven't. But we've made a start and talking about the issues and helping each other where we can, is so important. And anyone who is feeling very low, or is struggling, must seek professional help. This could be a GP, a leader of a particular faith group or a helpline, including the Samaritans, for examples, on 0330 094 5717.

Anyway, it's now time to move on the next chapter: **A** for **A**chievement.

A for Achievement

Achievement is an interesting concept because, whilst it can relate to **something being done successfully** with effort and determination, and/or skill, and/or courage, and for which **a material benefit is gained**, success can also have **a powerful impact on the mind**.

Well, that's obvious.

OK. Feeling good, having a sense of satisfaction, feeling proud, and even feeling a sense of justification, are all good for our sense of well-being.

And why? Because achievements **are the building blocks** that enable us **to construct in our minds** a feeling **that we are a successful individual**, which is so important for our prospects in life. So, in terms of success (but not relating to human beings) let's read a poem about a spider.

A spider!

Yes. Just a simple spider. The poem is entitled, **Determination**.

Determination

I had a dream the other night that opened my eyes. I saw a spider on its web, waiting to catch some flies.

Then a bird flew by, and with its wing damaged the spider's web. Did the spider give up, not at all, it started to spin again.

The web was replaced in no time at all, but this time it was rearranged, it was as if the spider had worked things out and decided to make a change.

Let's talk REACH

Then the bird flew by, but out of reach, the spider's web survived, and the spider once more, with determination, waited to catch some flies.

I like the poem, but what's your point?

It's simply this:

In life, all sorts of things have a habit of getting in the way of our progress (our achievements). There are obstacles over which we have little control. Money and opportunity, for example, and as I have acknowledged before, many people who struggle with life's challenges may not have **the ability**, **energy**, **support** or **mental health** to enable them to make the effort needed to behave differently, **even if they wanted to**. But could it be that we just don't have **the confidence required to make the effort**, and for all sorts of reasons.

I know that a spider wouldn't have the same kind of negative thoughts and worries to deal with that a human being might have (well, not as far as we know anyway), but being a spider can't be that straight forward.

So, ask yourself this:

Do we really have any excuse **for not making a little more effort** to overcome **setbacks, disappointment, self-doubt** even, **which might be affecting our achievements?** If a spider can do it, surely, we can.

And I'm not talking here about improving our own life through selfish gains; we are all capable of this. No, the question you may need to ask yourself is this: **Are you sure?** Are you sure that you are not denying yourself the opportunity to do your best?

I know that asking this question may not be relevant to yourself, but it could be relevant to someone you know, if you know what I mean? So, let's read the following poem entitled, **Are You Sure?**

A for Achievement

Are You Sure?

How do you know what you're capable of; how can you be so sure? How many times have you told yourself you're not capable of anymore?

Is it about what's passed you by? Wasted school days, wasted time. Is it this that's getting you down, or is there something else that's on your mind?

You're older now, a different person, but are you still unsure? Get a grip of yourself, turn your life around, don't close an open door.

It will obviously take some effort, and it may even drag you down, but if in the end you achieve your goals, you might even feel quite proud.

So, now you've got the message, now you know the score, sort out your life, don't mess it up, go through that open door.

With the above in mind, let's give some thought to **the achievement journey**.

You've lost me again; explain.

Achievement journeys of every kind **begin in the mind** and rely on one's **ability** and **determination** to carry out the required processes.

OK.

Achievement is possible if:

a) We have a desire to achieve 'whatever'.
b) We think about and plan what we need to do, to make the 'whatever' happen.
c) We put into action whatever we have planned.

Let's talk REACH

Yes, that's obvious.

But (and this probably doesn't apply to you either), some people could benefit, in terms of achievement, if they could learn to **think differently**; occasionally.

Think differently?

Yes. Consider different explanations and possibilities to those that dwell in the mind the result of past experiences or influences. The following poem explains this quite well.

Achievement Happens

Achievement begins to happen in the mind, when thinking differently has arrived, and where thoughts, often deeply ingrained, no longer our positive actions do restrain.

Refreshing fountains wash away destructive attitudes that once did stray, releasing from bondage the captive hawk, to spread its wings, and with determination release a new creative imagination.

But when it happens, don't cast it out, don't stifle your beliefs with excessive doubt. You're made a start; you've displaced the demons, now expand your horizons with great achievements.

So, let's be clear. Whilst **an achievement of a practical nature** is an admirable 'result', never underestimate **achievements in the mind** because, as the poem suggests:

Achievement begins to happen in the mind, when thinking differently has arrived, and where thoughts, often deeply ingrained, no longer our positive actions do restrain.

A for Achievement

So, just to be a bit different, and to test your ability **to think differently**, give some consideration, not to a specific achievement that you might personally have in mind, but **to a problem that faces the whole of mankind worldwide**, the survival of planet Earth.

Are you sure that this is going to be helpful?

I hope so. See what you think by reading the following poem. It's entitled, **The Planet Speaks**.

The Planet Speaks

I speak, but you do not listen, I cry but you do not hear, my oceans are polluted, so too is my once-fresh air.

Wildlife is on the brink, because habitats no more supply the nutrients, water and shelter, upon which all creatures do rely.

The planet's getting warmer, and for some that may sound fine, but unfortunately that's not true for all, drought is destroying lives and habitats worldwide.

The human race in early times, despite their evil ways, didn't decimate the planet's resources or plunder for financial gain.

Today's problems are the result of mass production, over consumption, resultant waste and serious pollution. We either sort it out, or just die out, whichever is our preferred solution.

Achievement can be a dirty word if it results in world destruction, but if it benefits me (the planet) and you (its inhabitants) then that's a step in the right direction.

Let's talk REACH

OK, this poem has opened a whole new can of worms, demanding a whole new level of thinking.

I haven't heard that saying for a while, 'a whole new can of worms', but you are absolutely right; very challenging.

I just thought that reading a hard-hitting poem related to our home (planet Earth) might emphasise the importance and value and need to think differently and 'outside the box'.

The poem suggests that **overproduction, overconsumption, the use of and the disposal of products of an infinite variety, is where the problem lies**, in terms of the planet's survival.

And if you are in doubt about this, read the next poem (or rap) related to '**economic growth**'.

Economic Growth

Economic growth, GDP; what's it all about, one, two, three?

One is for Production,

Two is for Consumption,

Three is for Pollution,

Now let's see!

Economic growth is driven by production, goods and services and more money in the system.

Greater production means more consumption, energy, resources and land destruction.

A for Achievement

More consumption means greater pollution in the air that we breathe and in every other location.

Without our intervention and a change of direction, planet Earth is likely to experience total annihilation.

It's down to human beings in every situation, to play their part and begin the restoration.

Mankind needs a revelation to inspire every nation's regeneration.

Maybe we need to start a revolution, leading hopefully to a permanent solution.

Well, how does this make you think? How can mankind begin to **achieve differently** by **thinking differently** with the aim of sorting out the mess we are in?

I think that 'the mess we are in' is an understatement. Drought, wildfires, water pollution, contaminated land, the destruction of the rainforests, loss of Antarctic habitats, melting ice caps, coral reef destruction, and so much more, is more than just a mess, it's a planetary disaster.

It is, and it must not be underestimated. But ordinary members of the buying public have little or no control over what is manufactured and made available through multiple outlets, including shopping centres and online. **The only influence we have is to control what we buy**.

But of course, this has implications for employment, standards of living, government borrowing, public services, investment, and so on. **I don't know the answer**, but there needs to be one. But what I do feel confident in expressing is this:

Let's talk REACH

If economic growth is correctly defined as an increase in Gross Domestic Product (GDP) which occurs through an increase in consumer spending or an increase in product production, **then the sentiments expressed in the above poem are correct.**

The problem is: **achievement**, in many people's minds, involves a better standard of life (understandably), which usually means having **the ability to possess more 'stuff'**: more gadgets, electrical goods, cars, and so on – and for the very well off, more luxury stuff.

While this all sounds good for 'the economy', it's not so good for planet Earth, as the poem above pointed out.

So, what's the answer?

I don't know the answer (or answers), but there has got to be some, because as politicians across the world keep telling us, **global warming** will destroy the planet if we don't act now.

But very few politicians are admitting that **overproduction and overconsumption are a large part of the problem** (well, not as far as I'm aware).

So, where do we go from here?

Well, the more people that are prepared to think about the issues, raise the issues and yes, think differently and come up with globally workable solutions, the better.

And regarding **the desire to possess more stuff**, the following poem makes a few valid points. It's entitled, **Implications**.

A for Achievement

Implications.

I saw a computer for sale the other day, it had a great specification. I nearly took out a loan to buy it, until my dad asked me if I'd considered the implications.

You've got a computer, he said, what do you need another one for? It's old, I said, I like this one, and it has the facilities to do much more.

But have you worked out what you need to spend, the interest rate is nearly 18%?

And what about the health of the planet; a lot of the problems are related to our buying habits.

OK Dad, you've got a point. Yes, I probably need to give it a little more thought.

It's not unreasonable for the person speaking in the poem to not want to defer their gratification. They wanted an up-to-date computer, and there's nothing wrong with that, is there?

Nothing wrong at all (maybe) providing they had:

1. Considered carefully the **financial implications** of the purchase.

2. Considered whether they were simply wishing to satisfy **a want** rather than **a need**.

Whether the young person had considered the consequences of our **'over-indulgent pursuit of material possessions'** in regard to their potential purchase, we do not know. But certainly, in times of financial difficulty, impulse buying should certainly be avoided.

Let's talk REACH

I've just thought of something very important to add to the argument.

OK.

Even if people living in the more affluent regions of the world could somehow be persuaded to consumes less (for the benefit of the planet), there are millions of people on earth whose standards of living are so low, that they have every right to expect more material possessions and a better standard of life in general.

I agree completely, and I don't have any answers for this issue either. Some people **in our own society** can reasonably argue that they deserve more, as the following poem suggests.

It's Not Unreasonable

I can't simply just accept what I can reasonably expect, because situations in life, and fairness, just do not have respect.

Do not have respect for one's personal situations: background, upbringing, or even one's education.

Do not have respect for ill-health or disability, unemployment, homelessness, and other forms of instability.

So, sometimes wanting more than one can reasonably expect is understandable, when your hopes and dreams have been suppressed.

Not least, in terms of family, the ones you must protect, more can be appropriate, if fairness is to exist.

Why should I be deprived when others have so much, is it what I've failed to do, or is it just bad luck?

A for Achievement

The concept of fairness and equality are raised in this poem, and I know that inequality is widespread in society and in the world in general, but like you, I don't have any of the answers.

Some might say that they (whoever) probably haven't worked as hard as I have, and therefore don't deserve to possess what I possess.

But it's not that simple, is it?

No. Past failures, missed opportunities, lack of opportunities, or just bad luck, could have affected an individual's ability to do better in life. The following poem reflects on one person's experiences whilst at school, which has caused the individual to feel a failure. Its entitled, **I'm a Loser**.

I'm a Loser

I found schoolwork a total farse. I was no good at English, maths or even art.

In science, I didn't have a clue and in practical lessons, I had no idea what to do.

Words on a page had little meaning, and to be shown up in class was so demeaning.

No wonder I messed about and caused disruption; it was the only way I could get any attention.

So, answer me this, what am I to do, I was no good at anything and that's the truth.

When you consider the kind of things that could go wrong or be less than favourable in our growing up years, it's not surprising that **giving up** in adulthood, or **resigning oneself to the mundane**, happens. But the consequences can be devastating.

Underachievement in the mind is so destructive. It can create a feeling of hopelessness, disadvantage, unworthiness, low self-esteem, and so on, which can have huge implications for anyone's prospects in life and, especially their mental health.

Indeed, the following short poem illustrates **how destructive low self-esteem can be**. It's entitled, **It's My Fault**.

It's My Fault

I know it's me, it's in my mind, where troubling thoughts and fears reside. Thoughts about my value and worth; nothing good, it's a draining curse.

Feeling hopeless, havoc wreaked, but it's all my fault, because I'm weak. Confidence, I have none; I'm a waste of space, that's what I am.

Respect myself, there's none of that. I hate myself and that's a fact. Leave me alone, don't waste your time. There's no way on Earth that I can shine.

I feel sorry for anyone for whom life has little value and has lost hope (as expressed in the above poem), but it's almost certainly not their fault.

I agree, and we will discuss this more in the chapters that follow. It's almost certainly a mental health issue, and no one should feel this way. In terms of mental health, anyone who can break free from the clutches of self-doubt could justifiably say: I have made progress, I have achieved.

A for Achievement

Consider this: A computer that does a remarkable job has to contain a remarkable program to make the magic happen. In the same way, for humans to do a remarkable job – to feel good about themselves and function as happy and confident individuals – requires **their programming**, derived from experiences whilst growing up, to be as 'good' as possible. But, **through no fault of our own**, it's often not.

And then there are those **irrational thoughts** that we can generate as we inappropriately **compare ourselves to others**. No wonder **our value and worth** sometimes comes into question.

I understand all of this, but how can someone with very low self-esteem break free from the clutches of this destructive force?

Good question.

We are all different, and our circumstances will be different, and not surprisingly, therefore, our approach will need to be different. But the bottom line is this: **achievement in the mind** is what's required.

Achievement in the mind – go on.

Breaking free from the clutches of self-doubt (if this afflicts you) must take place in the mind, because that's where the issues lie (obviously). If you can react to your 'irrational thoughts' **differently**, resulting in an **'improved sense of well-being'**, then you can justifiably say, '**I have achieved**'.

This might require the help of a professional therapist or it could be achieved with the help of a friend, a family member, a partner, **or maybe just on our own**.

Here are some 'self-help' suggestions:

First of all, recognise **what you are good at**; everyone is good at **something**. Then, when and where you can, use this **something** to

Let's talk REACH

your advantage in your social interactions and in other situations in life.

That's all very well but lo...

Yes, I was about to say, low self-esteem or lack of confidence can often result in an individual **avoiding social situations** altogether, or not contributing or engaging effectively whilst in company.

As understandable as this might be, it's so important to try to change this behaviour. So, if there is someone you know who does struggle with any of the above, help them to integrate back into social situations where they can feel a degree of comfort and, in particular situations, where people are not likely to be judgemental.

And then there's self-image.

We probably all look in the mirror on a daily basis and think, 'whatever', but be realistic about your appearance (your looks). Don't compare yourself to celebrities or other stand-out figures in the media. **Just look around at a 'normal' group of people when you are out and about**. You will soon realise that human beings are **an infinite mix** of shapes and sizes and with all sorts of peculiarities, characteristic and features. OK, some will try to 'make a big statement' appearance-wise, whilst others will just relax and be themselves, and this, in the main, is how most people present themselves.

And then there are those **negative beliefs** which can so easily affect our self-esteem. It's so important **to identify and acknowledge these.** Then, with common sense, **challenge those beliefs**, because **no one is perfect** and no one is as confident as they appear to be. Sometimes it's just an act.

To do the above you are going to have to **talk to yourself** (out loud, if necessary), and **explain to yourself** that you are what you are, **and being you is OK**, because whilst you may have blemishes – physical

A for Achievement

or emotional – **you can become more OK in your mind**, where it matters. Remember, success and achievement, and the satisfaction gained, **is not just about material things**, it is about **how you feel about yourself as an individual**, and how you navigate this confusing and bewildering world.

Everyone will have their own priorities, **the things that could make them feel better about themselves**. So, do any of the following appeal?

- Being more friendly.
- Being more helpful.
- Being more considerate.
- Being more confident.
- Being more assertive (but in an unprovoking way).
- Being more relaxed and at ease.

These are the kind of **achievements** that will boost your sense of well-being because, **in your mind,** you will begin to feel **that you are a person of worth**, and very quickly, **others will feel the same about you too**.

It's clear, from all that we have spoken about above, that achievement has many connotations, as the following poems summarises. It's entitled, **Let's Be Clear**.

Let's Be Clear

Daily life is a tapestry of things we think or say or do, but what determines their renditions will be unique to me and you. Unique because the factors that play into our hands will be, to some extent, determined by our own desires and plans.

So, life, in essence, is a journey, motivated by the need to achieve; there's little else that drives our presence, it's just wanting to succeed.

Let's talk REACH

And let's not underestimate what achievements can achieve, not least, for the human spirit, a sense of purpose, confidence, and self-esteem.

But equally, we must not forget the damage that can proceed, not just when our achievements disadvantage others, but also the planet's needs.

So, in this life-long journey our responsibilities are huge, not only for our own success and happiness, but for all other causes too.

Of course, without striving for achievements, life on Earth would not progress; even if human beings didn't exist, nature would rely on this.

It's just a matter of balance, the way nature sorts things out. Well at least it did until mankind put the spanner in the works.

Whilst everyday achievements are clearly important to the individual and the continued existence of planet Earth is important to everyone and every creature that lives upon it, you would think that we might put more effort into sorting things out – personal or otherwise.

Well, at least most of the world's nations are taking climate change seriously and are taking steps towards reducing the emission of greenhouse gases and the disastrous effects of global warming.

True, but whilst this **might benefit planet Earth** in terms of **global warming**, if we continue to produce and consume more stuff, then the problems **related to pollution** will continue – and we might even **run out of raw materials**.

So, we need to recycle more?

A for Achievement

We do, but many products are made from a mixture of materials and components that cannot be easily separated and therefore recycled.

But a lot of recycling does take place, and we (the general public) can help by putting in more effort to recycle the products we use, or repurpose them where we can. And manufacturers need to be more 'planet aware' during the design and manufacturing process.

Absolutely, and if we continue to decimate the rainforests, and other important habitats, for raw material and other uses, **the oxygen-producing trees** will not be there **to provide the oxygen we need** in the air that we breath.

This is all sounding very depressing!

It is depressing, but part of the answer has got to be **that we all consume less**, and, as the above poem suggests, take a leaf out of nature's book:

Of course, without striving for achievements, life on Earth would not progress; even if human beings didn't exist, nature would rely on this.

It's just a matter of balance, the way nature sorts things out, well at least it did until mankind, put the spanner in the works.

Finding **a balance** by deciding **what our priorities** are and **what we can justify**, whilst **protecting our home, planet Earth**, has got to be part of the answer.

You only need to read the poem (or rap) **Economic Growth**, to be reminded **that our achievements** (in terms of creativity and enterprise) have had, and continue to have, huge consequences for planet Earth and all of its inhabitants.

But the human need to achieve will never diminish, because it drives the human presence, as expressed in the above poem.

So, life, in essence, is a journey, motivated by the need to achieve; there's little else that drives our presence, it's just wanting to succeed.

So, how can we satisfy that which drives our presence, in other words, achievements, in ways that are less destructive?

I'm listening!

Well, this is one suggestion. **Because achievements are the building blocks that enable us to construct in our minds a feeling that we are successful individuals**, then maybe concentrating more **on our feelings** and their **consequences**, and not **our possessions**, and their **benefits**, could be a way forward.

Whilst having stuff that makes life better, more comfortable, more enjoyable, and so on, will always be desirable (nobody wants to go back to living from hand to mouth in a damp, cold cave), it doesn't have to be such a big issue in our lives, does it? Consumerism (by definition) leads to consumption, and consumption leads to overproduction, and overproduction leads to waste and pollution, as expressed in the poem (or rap) Economic Growth.

So, what was I about to say? Oh yes.

Life, in the more affluent regions of the world, offers countless opportunities for enjoyment through achievements which do not have to involve gaining more possessions: buying unnecessary luxuries, etc. For example, just having a sense of satisfaction and a feeling of well-being can be created by:

- Being out and about and socialising with friends and family in the countryside, and many other locations of interest.

A for Achievement

- Pursuing creative activities that provide a sense of achievement.
- Being the kind of person that other people like and value, because then we are more likely to like ourselves, and that is a most valuable achievement.

OK, it's now time to move on to the next chapter: **C for Comfort**.

C for Comfort

When you think about the complexity of the human body, with it numerous biological functions and physical abilities, it's no wonder that **comfort** is so important in our lives, as the following poem begins to explore.

Comfort Pains

When thinking about life's comforts, so many factors you can find, because comfort exists not only in the body, but also in the mind.

It's no surprise that physical needs might at first appear to top the list. Because the body is so incredibly complex, pain almost anywhere can exist.

But even when the body feels fine, the mind can take a hit, in fact its troubles can be so deep, that maybe they should top the list.

Troubled thoughts, things unsaid, or things we should have said instead. Mind in turmoil, comfort threatened, if our thoughts cannot be settled.

But we can't dismiss the physical hits; not to name a few would be remiss:

Headaches, toothaches, backaches, cuts and bruises, stomach aches, coughs and sneezes, not to mention the more serious conditions and diseases.

Comfort is clearly a powerful factor, that in our personal lives can really matter. But, of course, the comfort of others too, can be down to what we actually say or do.

C for Comfort

So, what exactly is this poem suggesting?

Well, firstly that comfort (or discomfort) can affect our own bodies and minds, in all sorts of different ways (obviously) and as the poem points out, comfort:

...is clearly a powerful factor, that in our personal lives can really matter.

But equally, we are reminded that:

... the comfort of others too, can be down to what we actually say or do.

Physical discomforts can be (but are not always) the easiest to deal with. They most often affect just oneself, unless we depend on Mum and Dad, a carer, a partner, a friend, or a healthcare professional to help or support us; and they may have to shoulder some of the challenges and responsibilities.

Discomforts in the mind are often much more difficult to deal with because **not only** can they impact on our own sense of well-being and mental health, but very often, they can have a significant impact on others too.

In our daily lives, there are so many different things going on physically and mentally (on a minute-by-minute basis), that **even when we feel OK**, we can, **without realising it, cause other people discomfort**, and this is not good.

For most people in life, there are concerns and troubles, worries and anxieties of an infinite variety that need to be dealt with on a daily basis, and very often, just by themselves. Do we therefore (any of us), have a right to increase other people's discomfort by our own poor behaviour? Let's give this some thought.

Let's talk REACH

We will not discuss here the behaviours of those extremely thoughtless individuals who abuse others in the ways described in the Relationships chapter. I hope that any reader to whom this applies has already spent some time reflecting.

I'm thinking, at the moment, about behaviours that, for some people, are not even recognised as 'an issue', but just every day, casual, matter-of-fact ways of behaving.

For example:

Impatient behaviour **when driving**. Selfish behaviour **when queuing**. Loud behaviour **when socialising**, antisocial behaviour **when just out and about**, and so on.

Other people's comfort matters. It matters because, unless you are (which most people aren't) a selfish, thoughtless individual, for whom only your own existence is important, then striving for everyone's comfort (for all that this involves) can only benefit everyone.

That said, there are, in life, quite a lot of people, young and old, **who struggle to accept or tolerate other people's quite reasonable behaviour**, in all sorts of situations.

The list below illustrates a few examples:

- Long supermarket checkout queues, caused by **other people** being too slow, **in their opinion.**
- People driving more slowly **than they want them to.**
- Delays, of any kind, cause by **other people's** inefficiency, **in their opinion.**
- **Other people** making mistakes **that they wouldn't make.**
- Something being carried out **that doesn't meet their satisfaction or expectation.**
- **Someone else's** poor planning, resulting in **a waste of their time.**

C for Comfort

It's clear, from the above, that all sorts of human behaviour can irritate and annoy some people or make them feel uncomfortable at times.

But quite different to the above, some people are uncomfortable in company (as previously mentioned). Some are uncomfortable in the learning environment (schools, colleges and universities). Some are uncomfortable in the work environment, and the following poem has a few more things to say on the subject.

The Comfort Journey

It's not surprising that we strive to experience comfort in our everyday lives, because in mind and body dwells our essence: the very thing that defines our presence.

If on this planet we lived alone, the comfort journey would be just our own, but that's not the case, that's not how it is; in isolation we do not live.

Our own comfort, therefore, and those to whom we relate, and even those we rarely meet, is indefinably linked to what we say and do, or think.

So, let's be clear, make no mistake, we have a responsibility of the highest stake. Our existence with others is so entwined that our very being can their lives define.

No one is perfect, we know that's true, even the best of humanity has failings too. Carelessness, jealousy and selfish actions can sometimes generate unwelcome distractions.

And in times of uncertainty and financial difficulties, it's understandable to protect our own self-sufficiencies. But our own comfort should never be a snare to other people's comfort anywhere.

Let's talk REACH

So, where we can and if we are able, let's ensure that comfort for all is enabled, because comfort has such a powerful influence on the human existence and its deliverance.

I like the poem. It makes it very clear that we all have a responsibility of the highest stake to ensure that we (in every possible way) avoid making other people feel uncomfortable by our communications, reactions, or behaviours.

If only everybody could do this! What a difference it would make.

If we could all give a bit more thought to our communications, reactions and behaviours when interacting with others, e.g. friends, neighbours, partners, strangers, doctors, nurses, paramedics, the police, care workers, shop assistants, and so on.

I think we get the point – everyone.

The problem is: people have all sorts of **reasons why** or **excuses for** not relating well to others.

Some of the reasons could be described as valid, others, not at all valid. But can there really be any valid reasons, for any of us making someone else feel uncomfortable or wretched?

To begin to answer this question, let's have a look at a range of **reasons why**, or **excuses for**, one person (potentially) behaving unpleasantly towards another.

Selfishness	Revenge	Disappointment
Anger	Dislike	Disrespect
Intoxication	Jealousy	Frustration

C for Comfort

But, in truth, none of these are reasons for anyone behaving unpleasantly towards another, are they; even if your own comfort is being threatened in some way. For example:

You are driving on a 50mph stretch of road and someone who doesn't want to travel at the maximum speed is holding you up. You get frustrated, angry even, sound the hooter, tailgate, behave aggressively or even recklessly.

Is this an ideal way to respond to the situation?

You had arranged to meet a friend for an evening out together. You were waiting at home to be picked up. The phone rings. 'Sorry, can't see you tonight, a mate from work has just called round, see you tomorrow.'

Not the nicest of behaviour of a so-called friend. So how might you respond to this kind of situation, appropriately?

Let's see if the poem below, entitled, **Comfort Beckons**, shines any light on the issues.

Comfort Beckons

Comfort that's derived from interactions depends on mutual satisfaction. Give and take is what's required to ensure that no one is denied.

This relies on compromise, to ensure that mutual good feelings are supplied.

But it can't always be what we expect, because human beings are not that exact!

Personality, moral values, past experiences, double standards, all determine the human essence; so important when comfort beckons.

Let's talk REACH

So, all that human beings can expect, is that in our trials we do our best.

With thought, compassion and determination, comfort should be in consideration.

So basically, the poem is suggesting that within our personal interactions and because human beings are not 'exact' (don't necessarily have the same values, standards, life experiences etc.), it's not to be expected that we are going to always behave in the nicest possible way towards one another. Understandable, I suppose.

Understandable, yes, but as the poem also suggests, in our trials we (should) do our best (and) with thought, compassion and determination, comfort should be in consideration.

In other words, as has been suggested in the achievements chapter, **thinking differently**, rejecting old habits, old prejudices, old thought patterns etc. can make all the difference in many situations. Maybe that's what it's going to take, on some occasions, when considering our own and other people's comfort.

The following poem, entitled, **Does It Matter?** challenges the thought patterns of an individual who **might experience more comfort in their life** if they could begin to **think differently** about themselves and life's situations.

Does It Matter?

You've never had a confident smile, maybe you think it's not worthwhile. Do you only wish to compare your comfort with others who are in despair?

C for Comfort

Do you underestimate your talents and consider only your weakest assets? Why is your confidence in short supply? What has triggered this sad demise?

Maybe life has always been this way, comfort has eluded you or failed to stay. No comfort gained from satisfaction; no confidence inspired by other's reactions.

But now it's time to reject that journey, the way ahead must begin in earnest.

Comfort may be in short supply, but tell yourself, do not deny, it's just a matter of time and effort, so don't let despair your confidence threaten.

Let a new life be awakened, and let it be of your own making; a time to feel so much better, and let your old life no longer matter.

Yes – a lot to think about for someone who is feeling 'less than comfortable' in their life at the moment.

At this point, it might be appropriate to be reminded of the words to be found in the poem (previously read), **First Thoughts**.

Have you ever thought about how your thoughts first started out? Did you form them on your own? No, thoughts are rarely yours alone.

Life dictates how thoughts are formed, and in your memory, some are stored.

The point I am making (as the poem, **Does It Matter?** suggests) is that maybe (for whatever reason) their upbringing hasn't provided them with **comfort gained from satisfaction, or confidence inspired by other's reactions** in sufficient measure to give to them the mental

Let's talk REACH

energy to achieve their full potential. But the poem then goes on to suggest:

...let a new life be awakened, and let it be of your own making; a time to feel so much better and let your old life no longer matter.

Easier said than done, I suspect, for some people.

You are right, but if you believe that it's only fair for everyone to have the right to achieve a better life, then as the poem, **The Comfort Journey** states:

...we all have a responsibility of the highest stake to help others where we can, because our own comfort ...and those to whom we relate and even those we rarely meet, is indefinably linked to what we say and do or think.

So, with **what we say and do or think in mind**, let's consider three very different comfort situations which can impact on our lives:

1. When **not** being comfortable can be helpful.
2. The Comfort Zone.
3. Self-imposed discomfort.

OK, sounds interesting.

When not being comfortable can be helpful.

It was mentioned (in an earlier chapter) that **discomfort** as we react to information from the senses, **can keep us physically safe** in different ways, but in this chapter, I am thinking about **uncomfortable emotional experiences** and how they can protect us, warn us, or encourage us to behave cautiously. For example:

There are those **uncomfortable feelings** we sometimes get as a result of **our own actions**. Selfish behaviour, impatience, jealously, anger,

C for Comfort

and so on, are behaviours, that do us 'no justice', and which almost always have a negative impact on others. It's clear, therefore, that **not being comfortable**, in some situations, **can be beneficial**. But feeling uncomfortable in these situations is very much dependent upon our own **moral values** and our personal view **relating to 'right and wrong'**. I'll leave you to think about this one.

OK, now let's give some thought to:

The Comfort Zone.

The comfort zone – that 'psychological state' which provides a sense of security and often reduced levels of anxiety, is understandably desirable. But it can very often be a barrier to potential enjoyment or achievements in so many different situations. The following poem, **The Comfort Zone**, has a few valid points to make on the subject.

The Comfort Zone

It's a place of refuge, the comfort zone; it can be a shared experience, but you're often on your own.

Better to be there to avoid any complications, well at least that's how your mind perceives the situation.

But when you hear about the adventures that some other people have, does it make you envious, and even a little bit sad?

Maybe this should compel you to be brave and take a risk, but go with friends, be cautious, and experience what you would've missed.

And if things work out, your confidence will steadily begin to show, and very soon you'll notice a very different you.

Let's talk REACH

You'll then look back and realise just how much you've grown and feel so pleased that you closed the door on the restrictive comfort zone.

It can be **a big step** for some people **to close the door on the comfort zone**. So many factors can come into play where comfort is concerned, including negative childhood experiences, insecurity, past failures, low self-esteem, and personality traits too, all of which can have a bearing on one's ability to step out of that 'psychological state' which can be so 'comforting'.

Lack of confidence, fear of the unknown, reluctance to take even minor risks, can have such a negative effect on the potential for our enjoyment. So, as I have suggested before, try this: **make a decision to act, think about what could go wrong and how you could deal with the going wrong bit if it happened, then do it!**

OK, let's give some thought now to:

Self-imposed discomfort.

Sounds ominous!

Think about it. Sometimes we can cause ourselves **unnecessary discomfort by our own inappropriate responses** to all sorts of encounters, situations or events in life. The following poem makes reference to this and makes some suggestions. It's entitled, **A Peaceful Mind**.

A Peaceful Mind

A peaceful mind ignores distractions, those that promote unnecessary reactions. Reactions that disturb our feelings in ways that can be quite unappealing.

C for Comfort

Sights and sounds that have no relevance to a peaceful mind and its deliverance. And this includes other people's interactions, intolerances or quite deliberate actions.

So, if you can, and when you're able, discount the thoughts that discomfort enables. Because comfort thrives in a peaceful mind, which avoids unnecessary sights and sounds.

OK, but there are countless 'sights and sounds' that impact on our senses on a daily basis, to which we must respond, to enable us to deal with the situations or events that have caused them.

Absolutely, but whilst accepting that there will be in life innumerable decisions that we have to make, and which have the potential to cause discomfort, you have to wonder why some people **choose to add to their discomfort by reacting negatively to situations over which they should not be overly concerned**.

Clarify what you are saying.

OK, there are all sorts of situations in life where someone **we don't even know**, in **situations that are not of our making**, behaves **selfishly or inappropriately**, and in which we have **no opportunity to intervene**.

So, my question is this: should we allow **situations like this** to create discomfort in our minds?

Well, it's unavoidable, isn't? If the behaviour, in question, irritates you, annoys you or angers you, then discomfort happens, and we have little control.

If we have, as you put it, 'little control' then yes, the discomfort happens. So, the next question we need to ask is: **is having little control inevitable?**

Let's talk REACH

This is getting a bit technical; I'm not sure we can answer this.

I agree, and to get a comprehensive answer we would probably need to speak to an expert (unless you are an expert). Even so, I think that together, even the non-experts could come up with some common-sense suggestions.

OK, so what kind of things might cause someone to display irritability, annoyance, anger, and so on?

Well, here are some suggestions.

There are all sorts of **personality traits** that **could** affect an individual's degree of tolerance to distressing situations. But we will have to leave this one to the experts.

Past experiences of a similar nature **might have a role to play**. The subconscious mind has access to all sorts of information stored in our memory that **could** be used to influence our responses or behaviours.

Stress, resulting from any number of life experiences, **could** affect some people's tolerance to other potentially stressful situations.

Health and **well-being issues**, of an infinite variety, **can** affect how anyone is likely to react to 'normal' situations in life, let alone out-of-the-ordinary situations.

From all that you have said above (and this is probably only just scratching the surface of the subject), then having little control is probably inevitable?

But can you see **the irony** in the situation? Stress or anxiety-provoking issues that might be creating discomfort in a person's mind (as suggested above), can serve to **generate further discomfort** as the individual responds **unnecessarily** or **negatively** to **another** situation.

C for Comfort

Surely, there has to be some possible remedies for this dilemma.

You would hope so, but maybe we will not be able to take this any further, other than to say: some people may have to accept that **if** they are unable to control their unnecessary and unproductive outbursts, then **maybe** they should try to get help from a professional therapist.

On the other hand, some people might be able to say, **yes**, I do recognise that I am allowing myself to get unnecessarily over-distressed or over anxious in some situations that shouldn't be distressing me, and **I'm going to put in some effort to change things**.

So, to anyone in either of the above situations, it might be helpful to keep the first and the last lines of the above poem in mind:

A peaceful mind ignores distraction, those that promote unnecessary reactions.

And:

... comfort thrives in a peaceful mind, which avoids unnecessary sights and sounds.

So, **in conclusion** (and before we move on to the next chapter), let's be clear:

- **Comfort** in mind and body can have a huge impact on our ability to form, enjoy and maintain many different kinds of **RELATIONSHIPS** in our lives.
- **Comfort** in mind and body can have a huge impact on our **ENJOYMENT** in life.

Let's talk REACH

- **Comfort** in mind and body can have a huge impact on our ACHIEVEMENTS in life.
- **Comfort** in mind and body is fundamental to all aspects of our HEALTH.

H for Health

The last sentence of the previous chapter states that **comfort** in mind and body is fundamental to all aspects of our HEALTH and this is reflected in the first line of the poem, **The Comfort Journey**, which reads:

It's not surprising that we strive to experience comfort in our everyday lives, because in mind and body dwells our essence: the very thing that defines our presence.

Our essence: the very thing that defines our presence!

Yes, it's a very appropriate word, **essence**. It is defined as: **the intrinsic nature or indispensable quality of something**.

That says it all when thinking about the complexity of the human body with its numerous biological functions and physical capabilities, and the poem below puts it quite well too.

The Body

The body and mind will not be perfect, it's not something that we can expect, but still, it's an extraordinary structure that should demand our deepest respect.

Its level of sophistication will be beyond our understanding, unless we work in the medical profession, and acquire the skills and knowledge demanded.

Nevertheless, we owe it to ourselves, a level of comprehension, to enable us to look after our health, in body and mind, and pay it some serious attention.

Let's talk REACH

Good health, of course, is like a lottery, a random chance not clear to see, but when we have the opportunity to choose, it's down to us not to abuse.

Our health, of course, our choice (respected) but get it wrong will we accept it. We know the risks we're taking, of course we do, there's no mistaking.

Some very good points expressed in this poem, so where do we start?

Well, let's see if we can get a 'level of comprehension' to enable us 'to look after our health, in body and mind', and let's begin with **the air that we breath**, and let's start with a poem, entitled, **Breathing**.

Breathing

When we take a breath to fill our lungs with air, we can often take in substances of which we are unaware.

Good clean air is what we require, from which oxygen in the blood stream is derived. And then every cell in our body is enabled to produce the energy needed, to keep the body stable.

But we must be cautious, we must be wise, it can be so easy when ill-advised to pollute our blood stream and body tissues with substances that can cause all sorts of issues.

Vehicle exhaust gases, cigarette smoke, vaping fumes and other drug abuse, viruses from coughs and sneezes can all produce unpleasant conditions and diseases.

So, if we want to avoid unhealthy conditions, it can be about making sensible decisions. Sometimes it's about taking simple precautions and avoiding situations that can be damaging for us.

H for Health

So, could we all have better health, yes, with consideration and common sense. But some unfortunately will get it wrong, and a healthy life will be undone.

OK, so where do you want to go with this?

Well, I'm **not** going to say very much about **the dangers of smoking**, because people either:

- Know the dangers.
- Choose to ignore the dangers.
- Don't know the dangers – **and if this is the case**, someone needs to talk to them and explain.

For example:

Tell them about **the research** that suggests that people who start smoking in their teens and continue to smoke for two decades or more, **will likely die twenty to twenty-five years earlier** than those who never light up.

You could also tell them about **lung cancer, heart disease, stroke, impotence in males, cervical and breast cancer in women** – and so much more.

You would think that this kind of information would put anyone off smoking.

You would, and it has to some extent. You only need to visit appropriate Gov.UK and other internet sites to learn about the huge drop in the number of people smoking in the UK over recent years.

But let's be clear – the health issues related to smoking **have been know about for decades**, and whilst different governments have made some changes that have had an impact on the situation,

Let's talk REACH

many other organisations and private groups have played a huge part too.

That's brilliant; the fact that the number of people smoking has gone down in recent years, but cigarette smoking is being replaced with vaping.

Isn't that fantastic?

I know that you are being sarcastic – but I know what you are getting at and what your concerns are.

No one knows for sure (obviously) the percentage of teenagers and young adults who are currently vaping, but it's almost certainly much higher than some of the estimates we see in the media.

But what we do know is this: nearly all vapes contain nicotine. Nicotine is highly addictive and since the UK vape industry is worth £1.3 billion, there's a lot of this stuff about.

Listen to those who, in a very short period of time, **have become addicted to vapes**, and let them describe **some of the health problems they are already experiencing**.

Listen to teenagers who can tell you about **peer pressure**, and how despite **not wanting to start vaping**, they are 'pressured' into doing so because they don't want to appear different.

Not least, listen to **head teachers** who will tell you about the hugely disruptive effect that vaping is having on the educational environment in many different ways.

The psychological pressure on teenagers to be part of the 'gang' is huge. Anybody who knows anything about being a teenager: teachers, parents of teenagers, doctors, understand that peer pressure is one of the most powerful influencing factors in a teenager's life.

H for Health

I recently heard a politician talking about 'what could be done to discourage vaping'. They (whoever they were) were considering, apparently, making the packaging less attractive to young people.

That'll make a huge difference!

We are talking about teenagers here. Even if the packaging contained no graphics, no cleaver names, and lots of distressing facts, it would make very little difference – it's too late.

Adolescence is marked by a tendency towards risky behaviour and experimentation. To stop the vaping habit now would require some very decisive action.

But let's not worry about it!

In about ten years' time we will have some scientific facts to support our concerns. Then we can begin to sort things out.

And by then we will have potentially millions of people **addicted to nicotine**, and **who will have become addicted before adulthood**. And why is 'before adulthood' an issue?

I think I know why!

Because the teenage brain is still developing and continues to do so even into early adulthood. There's a lot of research into nicotine exposure, during this period, and its long-lasting effects. The cravings alone will become extremely difficult to overcome, and the vaper will not be able to give it up so easily.

And to make it worse, many young people who may never have considered smoking at all will have become addicted to the vaping habit instead. Brilliant!

Let's talk REACH

These issues, I think we agree, need serious consideration and fast action. Some countries have already made vapes available only on prescription. How long will it take for our government to act appropriately? This is clearly a very emotive topic which needs addressing urgently.

There are also all sorts of other drugs on the market, for which I have minimal knowledge but which I know can be hugely damaging to people's physical and mental health. But because I have no experience in this connection, I wouldn't like to get into a conversation about it, other than to say: any concerned observers (you or me) should do what we can to encourage, help and support anyone we know in any ways we feel able, whilst ensuring that our own safety is never put at risk. And, anyone should be able to get help from their GP which could include discussing the issues, being given advice, and being recommended treatment programs in their local area, and so on.

But let's move on and talk about some other nasties which can enter our bodies, and often without us even being aware, like **viruses**.

However, I don't think we need to say very much about **viruses from coughs and sneezes or through physical contact**, because I think most people are aware of how to avoid these – and the **Covid pandemic** has been a tough lesson for us all.

Absolutely, and our main protection (for those who have no objection) is vaccination where possible and available, and wearing a mask in indoor areas is a very sensible precaution – whilst the risks remain high.

OK, now let's now talk about food, something I know a little bit more about, and which can be another area of concern, **health-wise**, if we don't pay heed to the various health warning in the media and elsewhere.

Food, health warnings! You're not going to depress me, are you?

H for Health

I hope not!

Eating, for most people, is a pleasure. I say, 'for most people', because I know that there are many people who suffer with eating disorders, including binge eating, bulimia nervosa and anorexia nervosa, for example.

But for those **who do not have a diagnosed eating disorder**, the following poem entitled, **It Tastes Good**, still raises a few important issues.

OK. Let's hear it!

It Tastes Good

Despite the amazing 'goings on' inside our digestive system, we rarely give these processes any serious consideration.

It's what's on the plate or in the store: the smell, the taste and the looks, that we adore.

But if the digestive system had a say concerning the body's needs, many of the foods that we enjoy, it would rather we didn't eat.

The digestive system has a job to do. It's not a pleasure garden, its function is to maintain our health, but it can't avoid our own self-harming.

The problem is: lack of self-discipline or proper information can result in health conditions that can only be diagnosed with professional intervention.

So, we need to know some facts about the food we are consuming, and to take some steps to avoid ill-health, where self-discipline needs improving.

Let's talk REACH

So, in light of the above, let's see what we know about the foods we are eating.

I don't wish to insult the intelligence of those who are very knowledgeable about food, but for those who aren't, a few simple facts might be useful – so let's start with **carbohydrates**.

Food labels, with a similar format to the one shown here, are common on packaged food products. So, let's use this label as an example as we investigate.

OK, so what exactly are carbohydrates?

Carbohydrates are, in essence, 'sugars' and they provide the body with **energy**. All the cells in our body need energy.

Take a close look at the food label.

NUTRITION	per 100g	per pack	GDA adult	per pack
Typical values				
Energy kJ	450	1345		
Energy kcal	105	315	2000	16%
Protein	7.5g	23.7g	45g	53%
Carbohydrate	8.8g	26.4g	230g	11%
Of which sugars	1.2g	3.6g	90g	4%
Fat	4.2g	12.6g	70g	18%
Of which saturates	2.7g	8.1g	20g	41%
Fibre	1.2g	3.6g	24g	15%
Sodium	0.24g	0.72g	2.4g	30%
Equivalent of salt	0.60g	1.80g	6.0g	30%
GDA = Guidance Daily Amount				

This label 'tells us' that, within this product (this pack) the Carbohydrate – **Of which sugars** represent 4% **GDA**.

So, what's this all about?

Let's deal with GDA first. **GDA** stands for '**Guidance Daily Amount**' (the total of each ingredient that an adult should consume in any one day). Keep this in mind as you read on.

And why does the label state: Carbohydrate – '**Of which sugars?**'

120

H for Health

To understand this, you need to know that there are **three different types of carbohydrate** (three different types of sugars), and they all have **different chemical structures** (which you don't need to know about unless you want to).

Sugar, the carbohydrate which you probably put into your hot drinks and is found in biscuits, chocolate, breakfast cereals, fizzy drinks and many other products, has **a very simple chemical structure** which the body **can absorb very quickly and easily**.

This is great, if you need a quick burst of energy when doing exercise, for example, BUT the problem is, if the body gets more than it needs, or can use, the rest gets converted into fat, potentially leading to the body becoming overweight.

Look at the food label and you will see that the number of grams of carbohydrate (per 100g or per pack) is bigger than the 'Of which sugars' value.

The bigger value **is all three types of carbohydrate added together** – and two of these are less of a problem. **Starch** is one of them. It's found in foods such as bread, rice, potatoes and pasta.

Starch (because of its **more complex** chemical structure) **is digested by the body much more slowly** and can supply us with energy over a much longer period of time and is less of a problem with regard to fat.

That's good!

And **fibre** (the third carbohydrate) **doesn't get digested at all** (because of its **even more complex** chemical structure) but it has a very important job to do: it regulates the bodies use of sugar, helping to keep hunger and blood sugar in check.

Let's talk REACH

So, what kind of foods contain fibre?

Good question. Fruit and veg, wholegrain bread, wholewheat pasta and pulses (beans and lentils) all contain fibre.

Now let's give some thought to protein.

Protein is an important compound of every cell in the body. Hair and nails are mostly made of protein and our bodies use protein **to build and repair tissue, including our muscles**. Look at the food label again and check all the numbers related to protein.

And what kind of foods contain protein?

Protein is found in fish, meat, eggs and cheese, and in veg such as beans and pulses, for example.

And what about fat?

Fat is essential for many bodily functions, as well as being a source of energy. But one type of fat – **saturated fat** – is not good for use **if we consume too much of it**, but it is essential in small amounts.

Look at the food label and notice that the **'Of which saturates'** section is coloured red. Sorry, I forgot to say, not only are manufacturers legally obliged to provide the information we are talking about but they also use the traffic light system; red for high, green for low etc.

Whilst **saturated fat** is found naturally in many kinds of foods, it comes mainly from **animal sources** such as red meat, including beef, bacon and pork, and also dairy products, including full-cream milk, cheese and butter.

And then there's sodium.

H for Health

Sodium occurs naturally in many food products in the form of sodium compounds. But salt (sodium chloride) is also **added by producers** to act as a **preservative** in processed foods and often, to **make the ingredients taste less bitter.**

So – adding salt to make something taste less better than it actually is, is a bit of a cheat then, by producers?

Well, yes, you could see it that way.

Take a look at the food label again and you will see **how much salt has been added** over and above the natural salt content of the ingredients.

The body needs salt **in tiny amounts**. But beware: the amount of salt that can end up on your plate, when taking into consideration **the naturally occurring salt** (in some food items), and **the salt added to processed foods** as a **preservative** and for **flavouring**, can be considerable.

And then there's **fibre**, also listed on food labels. And fibre (as described above) is a carbohydrate. I don't think I need to say any more about it because its role in digestion, and foods that contain fibre, were mentioned above.

So, a quick look around a food label has, I hope, provided you with some basic information related to what we eat and why.

Anyway, chances are, some of you **prepare a lot of your meals from scratch** (as it were), using fresh produce. **This method of meal preparation,** if you have the **time** and if you **enjoy** preparing and cooking food, and if you can **afford** the sometimes more expensive fresh products, **is the best way to do it** because:

You have control over what you end up eating, avoiding the ingredients that are not particularly good for you, and the chemical additives that your body can do without. And, **providing you don't add any salt from the saltshaker**, you can keep your salt intake down. A diet high in salt (or sodium) can cause raised blood pressure, which can increase your risk of heart disease and stroke.

So, in terms of striving for a better life, when it comes to our **health**, in relation to **food intake**, then thinking about, and being knowledgeable about what we are eating, is so important.

I'm not going to go into detail, regarding health problems associated with 'food intake', other than to say, the conditions and health issues listed below are, in many cases, associated with eating too much of the 'not so good' food constituents.

Heart disease, diabetes, stroke, hypertension (high blood pressure), some cognitive problems (and other mental health issues), sleep issues, unwanted weight gain, obesity, some cancers and many more.

Many health conditions, including some of the above, are not associated with poor diet. Some can arise as a result of harmful habits, including cigarette smoking, vaping, other drug use and alcohol consumption. If in doubt about any health conditions, speak to your GP if the problem is becoming urgent.

And since we haven't talked, specifically, about alcohol consumption, we probably ought to do this now – and guess what?

Another poem?

Absolutely. It's entitled, **Alcoholic Drinks**.

Alcoholic Drinks

Alcoholic drink in moderation, on a daily basis, or on special occasions, is an accepted part of social entertainment.

H for Health

Nothing wrong with that, you would probably agree, but in excess it can become a liability.

Like it or not, alcohol is a drug; it can help you feel confident in social situations and may produce a calming and relaxing sensation.

But, if overcome by alcohol use, you can make yourself very vulnerable and at risk of abuse.

It can also slow down the function of the brain, so if you're thinking of driving, that would be insane.

Addiction, of course, is not uncommon, both physical and psychological addiction can be a long-term problem.

So, avoiding these conditions should be your priority. Don't let the demon drink reduce your life expectancy.

So, just to be clear.

Alcohol, in moderation, can help people to **relax** and **enjoy** the company of others.

But because alcohol **can affect brain function, changing a person's mood and behaviour**, it can (sometimes) result in irresponsible reckless or even violent behaviour.

It can also make an individual **susceptible to being taken advantage of** either **physically** or **sexually**.

And worldwide, **3.3 million deaths** were attributed **to alcohol misuse** in 2012 (World Health Organisation 2014).

And just a few more points:

Let's talk REACH

Speed of alcohol consumption, gender, ethnicity and body mass, can all affect an individual's response to alcohol use, very differently.

And if you are in your **late teens** or **early adulthood**, the **brain is still developing**. This makes it (your brain) **more vulnerable to alcohol damage** than an adult brain.

So, **thinking differently** (if needs be) concerning alcohol consumption can be very important, **for our own health and safety**, and the health and safety of others too.

OK. We are nearly at the end of the book but there is one more hugely important issue we need to talk about, **mental health**.

So, what is mental health?

Put simply, **mental health is 'a state of mind'** determined by the processes taking place in the brain **that results in thought**. What actually 'goes on in our heads' to produce thought is hugely complex and doesn't need to concern us here, other than to say, it's these **'goings on'** in the mind that is the essence of mental health.

The 'goings on' in the mind?

Absolutely. Most people would probably say that their **mental health was 'good'** if they felt a general **sense of well-being**, and having a general sense of well-being usually means that they were dealing quite well, in their minds, with life's challenges.

And let's not forget, our sense of well-being is reflected in our **relationships**, the things **we enjoy**, the things **we achieve**, the things that give us **comfort** and of course, our **health**.

With the above in mind, let's read a poem entitled, **Mind Teaser**.

H for Health

Mind Teaser

Someone said inside your head were many contradictions, and when it comes to mental health this can result in all kinds of restrictions.

It's true, thoughts are absolutely essential for getting on with human life, but when our thoughts disturb us too much, our mental health can be on the line.

Thoughts are like a conversation, going on inside our heads, but when that conversation causes stress or anxiety, our lives can be filled with dread.

Some people appear so confident, easy going and self-assured, whilst others struggle with so many things which can sometimes sound absurd.

It may be a matter of motives, or even motivation, but it's our thoughts that drive these events, and these may need attention.

Is it our personality, intelligence or self-esteem, or is it just our emotions that we probably have to blame?

Maybe that's what it is, we're too sensitive or too shy, maybe we need to accept ourselves, exactly as we are.

So, is this the answer, is this the cure? No more pondering anymore. We're just as good as anyone else, so no more self-doubt, no more fretting, no more time spent regretting.

The last line of the above poem makes it all sound so easy. But, of course, it's not.

I agree.

Let's talk REACH

Self-Doubt, caused by bullying, racism, sexism, domestic abuse and a multitude of other issues, can result in despair, fear, and even loss of life, if not effectively addressed.

No more fretting. Easier said than done. It can take real strength of will to dismiss those distressing, and often frightening, emotional feelings.

No more time spent regretting. This, I suppose, if achievable, is good advice. All sorts of issues, however, caused by other people, different situations and even ourselves, can play on the mind and drag us down into the depths of depression.

It's clear, but not necessarily easy to achieve, **that we are mentally healthier** when we are '**in control**' and can respond '**successfully**' and '**appropriately**' to life's difficult, challenging and ever-changing demands. But we don't always process our thoughts in the most effective way.

What are you suggesting?

Well, the first thing to acknowledge is that we are all different and many different influences combine to make us who we are and what we are. Not surprisingly, these differences will almost certainly affect how we are likely to communicate, react, or behave in different situations.

That's true.

And, as the above poem suggests, **our thoughts** drive our motives and motivations, and maybe they need attention. And some people (as the poem also suggest) appear so confident, easy going, whilst others are less self-assured.

Clearly, **mental health is a complex, multifaceted 'condition'** and this is not surprising since life itself is complex (to say the least),

H for Health

and whilst **thoughts influence our emotions and behaviour, life's events influence both.**

So, if life is beginning to create feelings of desperation, what should you do?

The message as always is this: if you (or someone you know) is in serious distress, then seeking medical help (if appropriate), or even help from the police (in desperate situations) is what must happen. Alternatively, you might choose to speak to someone on a helpline. The Samaritans, for example, if you feel that this would be helpful, and speak to a trusted friend or family member in any situation to gain help and support.

But, if you think you can help yourself, then maybe you can, as the following illustrates.

Put very simplistically, human activity can be put into three categories:

1. The things **we enjoy doing** and **want to do**.

2. The things **we don't particularly want to do** but are **the necessities of life**.

3. The things **we have to deal with in life**, caused by unexpected events or difficult and challenging circumstances.

I'll go along with that, but what's your point?

Well, in the case of categories one and two we most often have the opportunity to **plan** for these events. **Planning** ensures (usually) that **we have what we need** to make what we want to do, or need to do, **more achievable**.

But what about category three?

Let's talk REACH

It's very difficult to plan for events or circumstances in the future **that we cannot possibly know about in advance** and **might or might not happen anyway**. And yet, these are some of the very events or circumstances that are likely to cause great anxiety when they occur and **could** be the instigators of potential mental ill-health issues.

Unexpected problems can arise, for a multitude of reasons, and many will be of a non-personal nature (i.e. practical). Your ability to deal with and resolve issues of this type, whilst remaining calm and avoiding stress, will be dependent on **you**.

Not a very satisfactory answer!

True – but I don't know you. I don't know what you are good at. I don't know what you are capable of. But what I can say is this:

Don't leave issues unresolved. Calmly and logically try to work out **what needs to be done**. Seek help, if this would be useful or essential. Come up with a plan and, to the best of your ability, work through the plan and try to get the issues resolved. But **never attempt anything that might put you in danger** (practically or otherwise).

Just remember: **unresolved issues are the ones that tend to trouble the mind**; the ones that can cause stress, anxiety and depression.

Whilst not knowing you personally, has (for obvious reasons) limited my ability to help you to sort out issues of a practical nature, we might, **together**, be able to shed some light on some **personal issues** which can on occasions, affect some people's **R, E, A, C** and **H** situations.

An example was highlighted in the poem (which we read earlier) entitled, **Critical Disclosure**. I refer to **self-awareness** and **emotional intelligence**.

H for Health

Clearly, as the poem highlighted, some people **do not have an appropriate self-awareness or a level of emotional intelligence** to enable them to recognise **how their behaviours might be affecting others**, and in some cases, professional help may be required. And in this connection, there is a diverse range of specialist services provided by therapists, counsellors and medical professionals to help those who need this kind of help, along with a multitude of other conditions.

But, with a bit of thought and effort, some people **may be able to help themselves** by 'getting personal' and asking themselves some tough questions.

The following poem could be used to make a start in this connection. It's entitled, **Ask Yourself.**

Ask Yourself

Ask yourself these questions, if you really are unsure. Is it me who's got the issues, or is there possibly something more?

Can I say I like myself, if not I must know why. Am I selfish or inconsiderate, I don't think that these apply.

Am I nice to be with, or do I drive them mad? Does my constant moaning make others feel quite bad?

Do I have a fixed mindset; only black or white? Some say I need to broaden my mind, not sure what they're talking about.

I'm told I fail to empathise when other folk feel sad, I don't know why that's such an issue, why should I make myself feel bad?

Do I actually know myself; am I self-aware? Do I have what they call emotional intelligence, and should I even care?

Let's talk REACH

Maybe it is me who has the issues, I don't know who I am. But if I need to sort things out, I may need a helping hand.

Whilst the concerns raised in this poem may not apply to you in any way, they could apply to someone you know who might benefit from your help. This however can be a difficult subject to address because the individual may find it difficult to accept that they have any issues that might be affecting others negatively. But if they do, these need addressing for the sake of their own mental health and the well-being of others too.

This is getting rather personal! Well, some people might see it this way.

Maybe, but to identify something that you (or they) are concerned about that might be causing 'issues' and that might need sorting out, is so important where mental health and relationships are concerned.

OK, let's move on.

Since thoughts precede everything that we consciously do, then thinking about how our thoughts can impact on ourselves mentally is clearly very important.

Explain.

OK. Thoughts are absolutely essential for life, as we have acknowledged before, but thoughts that are responsible for our anxieties, do us no favours. With this in mind, read the following poem, entitled (not surprisingly), **Anxiety**.

Anxiety

Anxiety begins to do its rounds when thoughts disturb a peaceful mind. Uncertainty about 'whatever' can often taunt a troubled mind's endeavour.

H for Health

uncertainty has no respect; it leaves us not knowing what to expect. The consequences of something going wrong are often the issues that the mind dwells upon.

The things we might find hard to do, because we are not physically or emotionally able to. Sometimes things just don't work out; we've tried, we've struggled but couldn't get it right.

Feeling like, 'I don't know what', a failure, no self-belief, and that's our lot. Anxiety telling us that we can't cope. It's got its hands around our throats.

But no, anxiety can be defeated. We need to think differently about its meaning. Remap our thoughts with positive emotions; we must not accept our mind's negative solutions.

I know what you are probably thinking…

Yes, how can you begin to calm a troubled mind if you need to?

Not straight forward, obviously, because all sorts of issues, personal to yourself, will probably require a very personal approach.

That's not very helpful.

OK. Some people, in some situations, will use what is referred to as the **protective function**. In other words, **they anticipate the worst** so that if the worst happens, they can justify their thinking – but if things go well – that's even better.

Whilst this approach might suit some people in some situations, **it's far from ideal** because **the anticipation of 'whatever' going wrong can cause all sorts of anxieties**.

Let's talk REACH

A much better option is to have a Plan B to deal with the **going wrong bit** if it happens (as discussed previously). This should alleviate some of the worries because there's nothing worse than uncertainty. As the above poem states:

Uncertainty about 'whatever' can often taunt a troubled mind's endeavour. Uncertainty has no respect; it leaves us not knowing what to expect.

Maybe some of our anxieties are the result of unrealistic expectations and the concern that 'whatever' might not work out. For as the poem states:

The consequences of something going wrong are often the issues that the mind dwells upon.

But then we are told to:

Remap our thoughts with positive emotions; we must not accept our mind's negative solutions.

OK, we've thought about **anxiety** briefly. Now let's give some thought to **depression**.

You certainly know how to make someone feel – depressed!

Well, that's not my intention, quite the opposite. And sorting out any issues in our **R**, **E**, **A**, **C** and **H** situations can go a long way towards achieving an overall sense of well-being.

My last comment was a joke – you did realise this?

I did. Anyway, without further ado, 'whatever this means', let's read the next short poem about depression. It's entitled, **Depressed – Or What?**

H for Health

Depressed – Or What?

From time to time, I feel so low, and the things I once enjoyed I don't want to know.

Life can be so sad, and the daily chores become such a drag.

Tired and listless most of the time, nothing pleasant on my mind.

Depressed, I just don't know, but to my friends it's beginning to show.

From time to time anyone can feel low, it's not unusual, this I know.

So, maybe it's just a passing phase, I'll feel much better another day.

Depression can affect anyone, at any time, and for a whole range of reasons. But, for most people, it's likely to be only short-lived.

The problem arises when the depression doesn't lift and remains dominant for sustained periods, and this is when urgent medical help should be sought.

Visit the NHS website: **Symptoms – Depression in adults**, to alert yourself to **the phycological** and **physical symptoms** of **depression** and make an appointment with your GP if you feel that this is appropriate.

Mental health is hugely complex, and different conditions will affect people differently. That's why there are so many different specialists practicing in different branches of medicine and therapy, and if you believe that you need this kind of help and support, you must seek it.

Let's talk REACH

Even so, we are frequently told (in the media) that 'it's good to talk' and whilst the following three issues might require professional help at some point, some discussion here and now might be useful. I refer to sleep issues, hoarding and gambling.

These topics seem a bit random!

True, but we can't talk about everything.

So, do you have sleep issues?

No more than anyone else might experience from time to time.

And what about hoarding. Are you a hoarder?

Absolutely not.

So, do you have a gambling problem; is this what it's all about?

100% no.

I could have chosen any number of 'conditions' to talk about; these just came to mind for some reason.

Anyway, let's talk about sleep, or more precisely, lack of it.

Most people, from time to time, find 'getting to sleep' difficult, or even 'maintaining sleep' can be a problem. Either condition can leave you very tired, irritable, and so much more.

Read the following short poem, entitled, **I Can't Sleep**, and see if it raises any issues for yourself or someone you know.

H for Health

I Can't Sleep

It's on my mind, I can't settle down, sleep eludes me most of the time.

Nothing serious, nothing to cause alarm, but it's there and nagging all the time.

Mind in turmoil, sights and sounds, everything going round and round.

I should wake up feeling refreshed, but not for me, I get no rest.

Sleep hygiene, the bedtime routine, not always easy in a family scene.

Maybe I have a medical condition; need to sort it out with a qualified physician.

If you or someone you know, has sleep issues, you can contact **The National Sleep Helpline** on 03303530541 to speak to someone for help and advice. Their opening hours can be found on The National Sleep Helpline website.

There is also a lot of very useful information on the NHS website: **Sleep Problems – Every Mind Matters – NHS.**

Don't ignore sleep issues. Long-term sleep deficiency can contribute to many chronic health problems, including heart disease, kidney disease, high blood pressure, diabetes, stroke, obesity, and depression. Sleep deficiency is also linked to a higher chance of physical injury in adults, teens, and children. Furthermore, in the short-term, poor-quality sleep can affect one's mood, ability to concentrate and even the ability to learn and retain information. But don't take my word for it, ask the experts.

Let's talk REACH

OK – next topic: Hoarding.

Hoarding probably came to my mind because I know a couple of people who are hoarders, and I know how much they struggle.

Is this a common mental health problem?

Not common. Hoarding can be classified as a mental health condition in its own right, but people might also experience hoarding as part of another mental or physical health problem.

Whilst a hoarding disorder in the UK affects only a very small percentage of the population, many people who would never consider themselves to be a hoarder do have mild hoarding tendencies. A 'serious' hoarder, however, will almost certainly recognise a lot of the issues spoken about in the following poem.

Hoarding

I'm a hoarder, yes, and I'm not sure why, but without this stuff, I just can't get by.

It gives me comfort, it relieves my stress, but I know it causes such a horrible mess.

Anyway, I might need this stuff one day, it's just too difficult to throw it away.

They're things I need, my possessions; surely this can't be called an obsession.

It's all-consuming; I know the score: constricted space, disordered floor.

A toxic issue, I've been told before, a crippling lifestyle and so much more.

H for Health

Is it my brain, the way I am, do I see things differently to how others can?

If things go wrong and I need outside help, can't let anyone in, I just can't cope.

So, help me please, if you can. I need a sustainable, workable plan.

I know. Any hoarder reading this poem could rightly say:

'You don't know the half of it.'

Exactly, and that's why we need to leave this topic mainly to the experts. If you are a hoarder, have hoarding tendencies, or know someone who needs help in this connection, visit the **MIND** website: **Hoarding – Mind** for information, help, advice and useful contact details, and much more.

But let's move on.

I know that there are a multitude of mental health issues that need discussing, and in this short book we can only discuss a few. But I do think that some discussion on the next topic, **gambling**, could be very useful because it affects, in different degrees, millions of people in the UK (and around the world).

Throughout history, gambling has taken **many different forms**, and within many **different cultures**. But today, and for simplicity, gambling, in the West, can be identified in the following three categories.

At one end 'of the spectrum', gambling is approached **as a fun activity**, where the 'reward' is simply that of beating your opponents in a game of chance.

Let's talk REACH

At the other extreme, gambling involves **the prospects of a large financial gain**, but involves **the risk of a substantial financial loss**.

And between the two extremes, gambling is seen as a chance activity where a small financial loss is 'acceptable', whilst the hope of a substantial gain is possible.

It is within category **two** above, however, where most of the serious consequences lie. Gambling is described as **an additive disorder when it involves the compulsive urge to 'bet' despite the potential negative consequences**, which can be far reaching, life changing, and even life destroying.

Researched commissioned by a leading UK gambling charity, **GambleAware**, found that **problem gamblers** were six times more likely to have suicidal thoughts or try to take their own lives, and could be fifteen times more likely to do so.

It was estimated (in 2020) that there were approximately 3.5 million problem gamblers in the UK.

If you (or someone you know) falls into this category and help is needed, as an absolute minimum, access the **Help for problem gamblers – NHS** website, where you will find information, advice and appropriate contact details.

Massive profits are taken by the gambling industries every year. It is estimated that, in the United Kingdom, gamblers lose about £14 billion every year to the industry, and people **who are most socially and economically deprived are more likely to be affected**.

Add to this **society's costs** of dealing with **social harms** including joblessness, debt, and many associated mental health problems. But, as expressed above, **the cost to the individual**, the **victims** of this hugely damaging addictive 'habit', can be **mind-destroying** with potentially extremely serious consequences.

H for Health

Knowing how to help someone you know (or even yourself) who could potentially be on the gambling treadmill, will be down to your own efforts and determination to seek help.

But, just being a responsible parent may be what it takes to deter one of your children from one day being 'attracted' to this damaging practice.

If you are a parent of a young child who enjoys playing computer games, be warned. Many computer games are very innocent, but some are not. The following poem, **Confessions of a Reformed Gambler**, has a very important message for parents in relation to **some** computer games.

Confessions of a Reformed Gambler

When I was a young lad, eight or nine, I started playing computer games at home online.

Not the innocent ones that I'd played before, that allowed me to win an exciting game with a massive score.

No, these required me to make a stake, a payment that allowed me to build or make.

Not real money, just on-screen credit, but that, I believe, was the start of my gambling habit.

Not long after, I wanted more, so I tried the one-arm-bandit at the local store.

I started stealing from my mother's purse; I needed money and at the time I couldn't imagine anything worse.

When old enough, I progressed to the high-street arcade. It was there, I assumed, that real money could be made.

Let's talk REACH

But no. It was the machines that were making the killing, and to make it worse, I was always so willing.

It didn't matter at first because I'd got my first job. Whilst the income was helpful, it wasn't a lot.

After paying my way in the family home, there wasn't much left for any social time.

And then it hit me: I was addicted. The pressure, the anguish, I couldn't resit it.

My mind at last began to clear, no longer to this burden should I adhere.

And that's when I contacted Gamblers Anonymous. I'm recovering now, but it's going to be a very long process.

The poem highlights a series of events that **could** have led to a serious habit (an addition). But just in time it dawned on the individual that gambling was beginning to destroy his life.

Maybe his parents (or carers) should have been alerted to what was taking place, but it's not necessarily that straightforward.

To be aware of the many influences that the media, technology, and peers might be having on the thought patterns and behaviours of children, requires the adults to be extremely vigilant. Parenting is a hugely responsible role. Gambling is an immensely serious issue; we need to talk about it, and where we can do something about it.

But it's now time to move on to something else very important to our health, but a little easier to get our minds around, providing we don't try to get too cleaver: **Exercise.**

H for Health

And no! On this occasion, I don't have a poem.

OK.

Anyway, when we get active, our muscles begin to work harder and the heart has to deliver.

Deliver?

Yes. The heart has to pump more blood because our muscles 'demand more oxygen'. All the tissues in our body need oxygen, and oxygen is the fuel which provides the muscles with energy. But where does the oxygen come from?

From the air that we breath, obviously.

Absolutely, so this is how the lungs get in on the act. When we exercise, we have to breath faster to meet the increased oxygen demand.

Where is all this going?

Well, not much further actually, other than to say, all this increased bodily activity pays dividends in a multitude of different ways.

If you want to know how and why physical activity is not only good for our heart and lungs, but also how it can prevent weight gain, how it can reduce the risk of strokes, heart attacks, and many other physical and mental conditions, you will need to read a specialist book on the subject.

Oh, what a shame; I was beginning to get interested in this.

Sorry – anyway, back to the plot.

Being naturally 'beautiful' or 'handsome' is something over which we have little control (as previously mentioned), but we all, with the help of **exercise**, should be able to improve both our physical health and mental well-being. For example, people exercise:

- For **enjoyment**: a pleasurable, fulfilling pastime.
- To **relieve stress**: to lift the mood and create a sense of well-being.
- To **improve body image**: a slimmer waste, bigger muscles, etc.
- To **socialise**: to enjoy the company or others.
- To **lose weight**: if they want or need to.

Whilst exercise has many health benefits – some during the event, some immediately after the event, and some, very long-term – **lack of exercise** can have some **very negative health consequences**. For example, watching too much TV, playing video games for long periods, driving when you could walk and using an electric scooter rather than walking, are all sedentary lifestyle 'choices' which do little for our general health.

But we do have to acknowledge that, whilst exercise is a matter of choice for most people, for some, it can be problematic.

Being overweight, for example, and having certain medical conditions can be very restrictive. The advice, as always, is, if in doubt relating to potential problems associated to exercise and personal health, seek advice from your GP.

We are now getting close to the end of the book (and our conversations), but before we conclude, I would like to make a few more points which I think are important and might be useful.

At the beginning of this book, I stated that, in my opinion, **R**elationships, **E**njoyment, **A**chievements, **C**omfort and **H**ealth are **the basic ingredients of human life** – and this is still my view. But as the book has made clear throughout, **life** (in this context) refers to **all of us**, not just to ourselves, personally. And as the following poem makes clear, our **R, E, A, C** and **H** situations, **are indisputably connected**.

H for Health

REACH: The Indisputable Connections

Have you ever thought it out: what relationships are all about? Maybe we just take them for granted, with little thought regarding their advantage.

But without them life would not exist, because reproduction, would not take place. But it does, and new life in our hands creates new responsibilities and demands.

So why do things sometimes go wrong; why isn't all of life a blissful song? Because some couples experience troubled times, or relationships misaligned.

So how does enjoyment fit into the mix?

Well, clearly relationships are at their best when enjoyment for all can exist and when enjoyment is a compromise, and all involved feel satisfied.

But get it wrong through selfish needs, deceit or lies or other means, and enjoyment will be destroyed, and happiness will be denied.

So, while the potential for good outweighs the bad, some human beings can make life so very sad. With behaviours not consistent with joy, but rather pain, fear, anxiety, and intentions to destroy.

But let's not dwell on unpleasant behaviour, because joy and happiness can be our saviour. So, wherever we can, let's bring joy to each other's lives, and disregard those deeds that attempt to do otherwise.

And remember, when enjoyment is appropriately derived, it's most often through achievements that it will thrive. But achievement can be a dirty word, if in other people's lives, it makes things worse.

Let's talk REACH

But let's return to more pleasant thoughts and consider how achievements our comfort supports.

Achievements in personal pursuits, competitive events and educational routes, employment and family situations, all support our comfort needs, driven by enthusiasm and the will to succeed.

And as far as our health is concerned, comfort experienced in body and mind is a powerful force that cannot be denied.

Relationships, important, of course. Enjoyment, a driving force. Achievements, essential, couldn't agree more, and good Health, our energy store.

But what is the factor that supports all of these conditions? It's Comfort, of course, there's no room for omissions.

But not just our own comfort, that would be wrong; comfort for all makes society strong. So, maybe a change of direction, and thoughts redirected could results in society being better protected.

That was a rather long poem.

It was, I can't deny, but its aim was to show the **indisputable connections between** our **R, E, A, C** and **H.** and not only the connections, but **just how important comfort is** to everything else in the 'list'.

The problem is, despite having a supercomputer in our heads (our brain) which deals with the 'goings on' in our minds (our thoughts and emotions) minute by minute (well, much faster actually), we are not very good at seeing the whole picture. We tend to live our lives in the here and now and deal with one issue at a time.

H for Health

Anyway, if you agree that our **R, E, A, C,** and **H** are the basic ingredients of human life, then you might find the following analogy helpful in assessing the whole picture.

The Analogy

Picture for a moment a well-prepared meal; providing you with a tasty, healthy balance of nutrients.

To prepare that meal would require 'whoever' to use the best quality ingredients available. I bet you know where I'm going with this?

I think I do.

Now think of **life as a nutritious meal**. To be the best it could be for ourselves and everyone with whom we relate, or have any influence or impact on, all the ingredients required would need to be 'good' ingredients.

Some of the ingredients will be:

- Those 'dished out' by other people.
- Those which we supply ourselves.
- Those which we store in our mind's cupboard (our subconscious).

But some of **the poor ingredients**, 'dished out' by others, and often put into the mix by ourselves, can include:

Anger, selfishness, bitterness, envy, impatience, aggression, dominance, negativity, arrogance, laziness, rudeness, and so on. And there are also those ingredients **which can torment the mind** including:

Self-doubt, lack of confidence, shyness, low mood, anxiety, and so on.

Let's talk REACH

A lot to take in but keep talking.

A lot to take in, absolutely, and with all this going on, no wonder we fail to see the whole picture. No wonder life can get so messed up sometimes; life is just so complicated.

So, what's the answer?

Well, it's the 'goings on' in our heads where the answer lies.

Well yes, that's obvious.

And a very important part of these 'goings on' relates to our own and other people's **comfort**.

I understand what you are saying. Comfort in mind and body is the essence of a peaceful and calming presence within the human experience. But some people will strive to destroy this condition. I refer to the criminals and abusers of every kind. Hugely complicated. How can we begin to address this issue?

The first thing to acknowledge is that we are all **unique individuals**. The way we think and what we think about will be related to a multitude of factors related to our own circumstances and our consideration for others.

But, as a human species, deciding what is acceptable behaviour **for the benefit of everyone in society**, can only be arrived at with thought, discussion, consideration, and in some cases, protests. This is, and will continue to be, an ongoing process and we all, if we choose to, have an opportunity to take part. And, as individuals within our immediate sphere of influence, we may need to engage in this process, quite often.

The following poem makes a few suggestions in this connection.

H for Health

Why, What, When?

Distress can cloud our thinking, and often we're just not prepared to deal with difficult situations that arise, which cause us deep despair.

So, the question we may need to ask ourselves, before we get too depressed, is why has this thing happened and why are we so stressed?

Knowing why something has happened may become quite clear, but understanding why it happened, can be a much more difficult affair.

Was it me, or was it them; something missed, or something said; a situation unresolved, a difficult issue new or old?

Maybe something needs to happen to resolve the unpleasant situation. And if it does, we need to act, making sure that we know the facts.

So, the question 'what' next comes to mind, what would help the situation to unwind?

The course of action would much depend, on what's occurred and what needs to mend.

And once you're clear about what you know, then that's the time to 'count to ten' and ask the difficult question, when?

When should you make a stand; apologise, discuss or demand?

When feeling ready and able is the only time, when dealing with issues troubling the mind.

Let's talk REACH

The above poem implies that 'sorting things out' that are causing distress, will require action. Distress results in discomfort, and discomfort is, uncomfortable.

Feeling **uncomfortable in our mind** when we realise that **we have said or done something wrong, been offensive or less than constructive, can be disturbing. But on occasions, this kind of behaviour might need to be pointed out by ourselves to someone else**. The following poem entitled, **Comfort Matters**, illustrates such an example.

Comfort Matters

It's not my fault!

I think it is. You showed no concern for what you did. Their discomfort was clear to see, it was quite disturbing, I have to say.

But why should their comfort be of concern to me, what benefit could there possibly be?

You don't get it, you just don't see, how discomfort affects stability. Emotions disturbed by lack of comfort have the potential in life to cause disfunction.

As far as I'm concerned, I feel fine, and quite simply that for me is the bottom line.

But are you fine, are you really happy? Let me explain the comfort strategy.

Comfort works in two directions; get it wrong and there's disconnection.

H for Health

The mind, you see, has a memory store, containing past experiences, and so much more. These can determine our future actions, our communications and interactions.

So, what? That's the way life is; it's not a problem, it's the way we live.

But what you fail to understand, is that comfort has such a powerful hand.

It connects people's lives in a positive way, rather than creating disharmony. It communicates acceptance, rather than the consequences of rejection.

So don't dismiss the power of comfort, don't disregard its powerful function.

The latter part of the poem **makes two very important points**. Comfort …connects people's lives, in a positive way, rather than creating disharmony, and comfort communicates acceptance rather than the consequences of rejection.

So, nobody wins when discomfort is experienced or perpetrated.

Absolutely.

In terms of **the comfort spectrum**, there are those who cause **dis**comfort because they can be 'a pain in the neck', on occasions. These individuals sit at the lower end of the **dis**comfort spectrum.

Then there are those who cause **dis**comfort as a matter of course, as part of their chosen lifestyle (or even 'career'). These individuals sit at the higher end of the **dis**comfort spectrum.

And then there are those individuals who sit somewhere between the two extremes, some of whom we have talked about.

Let's talk REACH

And we all, like it or not, accept it or not, sit somewhere on that spectrum, and also like it or not, are in some way, or ways, **affected personally** by our **own behaviours**. For as the above poem points out, Comfort works in two directions; get it wrong and there's disconnection.

The recipient usually experiences the most pain in the first instance, but the perpetrator, somewhere down the line, will suffer as a consequence of their behaviours. This suffering will likely be as individual as the person experiencing it, but it will happen.

Maybe we all, therefore, need to spend a little more time trying **to think differently** about how we live our lives, how we communicate with others, how we interact with others, and how we behave towards others.

Whilst the poem, 'Thoughts' (earlier in the book), had quite a lot to say on the topic of thinking, it might be useful, if you accept that thinking differently might be important, to give it (thinking, that is) a bit more consideration.

Some thinking, naturally, takes place **as a result of what has just occurred**, and we react or respond accordingly. Does this thinking actually take place in the microseconds before we react or respond? Well yes and no.

Certainly, the brain, in an instant, is able to 'refer to' our experiences, emotions, attitudes, images, and so on (stored in our memory), and can use this information to influence our responses in whatever form is deemed appropriate, or otherwise, at the time.

Do we have any control over this brain activity at the time?

Not sure, you would have to do some research yourself if you would like to answer this question.

H for Health

But what is clear, I believe, is that **during periods of thinking**, when we are **just thinking**, and **not reacting to some outside stimuli**, we have the ability **to think differently** if we choose to. But that does require some degree of adaptability and being honest with ourselves; not just simply relying on old memories, experiences, attitudes, beliefs, feelings, emotions, images, and so on, established, generated, or imprinted within our minds throughout our lives.

And if we can begin to do this (think differently) then these thoughts will become part of the information available to the brain when needed in those moments before we communicate react, or behave. And as previously suggested, **pressing the pause button**, can be very beneficial.

Why?

Because pressing the pause button suggests that we are prepared to be more **patient**, and if we are more patient, we are more likely to elicit a more considered response.

Patience and tolerance have been referred to many times throughout this book and during our conversations, and in connection to a variety of issues within our REACH situations, haven't they?

They have – and why?

Because **patience** and **tolerance** are potentially very influential human characteristics. Many people's lives could be so much more **enjoyable**, more **productive**, less **confrontational** and, as a consequence, result in a greater overall **sense of well-being**, if our own, and other people's behaviours could be moderated, where appropriate.

The following poem quite graphically points out some of the negative consequences that impatience can have **on our health and well-being**. Its entitled, **Impatience Can**.

153

Let's talk REACH

Impatience Can

If you wish to damage your health, bouts of impatience can definitely help.

Sarcastic as this statement may be, it's there to remind us and help us see; to view the error of our ways and avoid its harm and darker days.

Stress and anxiety, caused by impatience, is not something of which we should be complacent.

The body's response to excessive stress, can leave our health in a serious mess.

Chronic stress robs the body of its protective function, and in its wake leaves tissue disfunction.

The immune system is often first to suffer, with all the consequences that this can offer.

The digestive system doesn't fare any better: upset stomachs and toilet bother.

And the reproductive system can take a hit, with all the problems that this can emit.

One of the most serious risks is heart attacks and strokes, it may sound inconceivable, but this is no joke.

So, is it worth adding to the stress that normal life has in its path, when impatience is our choice to make, are we really that daft?

Impatience, of course, not only has the potential to affect our own situations (within our own REACH experiences) but others people's too.

H for Health

But, if we are the kind of people who live 'decent sort of lives', then being **a bit more patient** or more **tolerant** (as appropriate) and **considering more often** other people's **comfort**, then everyone would benefit, I believe. I say 'appropriate' because being tolerant of other people's 'unacceptable behaviour', is clearly not a good idea.

Anyway, with comfort in our thoughts, read the following poem, which points out (as previously suggested) that comfort is a vehicle which provides an opportunity for the re-education of our thought processes and subsequent behaviours. It's entitled, **Better Times.**

Better Times

Comfort is a term that has many implications because it can relate to both physical and emotional sensations.

To be free of pain and in the mind calm thoughts sustain, will require for each a unique assessing, because we all have specific concerns that need addressing.

A time, maybe, to re-think our situations; lifestyle choices and even personal relations.

To achieve these states and feel the blessings, our thoughts will need to dwell in tranquil settings.

Where comfort can provide the conditions which can create in body and mind more pleasant renditions.

And empathy motivates our actions, to ensures that those involved gain satisfaction.

So, if a comfort journey needs attention new ways of thinking could determine its direction.

Let's talk REACH

And with a re-education of our mindful deliberations, we should be able to create for all more beneficial considerations.

So why not try to spend some time just thinking and considering if the way you (or someone you know) communicates, reacts or behaves, in different situations, could be 'modified', in some ways, for the benefit of those involved.

You certainly know how to put other people under pressure.

Oh dear, sorry! Anyway, since our **R, E, A, C** and **H** dimensions have featured throughout our discussions, let's read the penultimate poem that brings the REACH dimensions into focus:

The REACH Dimensions

Life is like, I don't know what; sometimes it is, and sometimes not.

Relationships are a point in question, managed well and they create a new dimension.

And Enjoyment can be a shared sensation if in body and mind respect is shown in all situations.

With Achievements being a success measure, in personal pursuits and in joint endeavours.

And with comfort dwelling in our bodies and minds, our Health should display fewer troubling signs.

So, all that we can hope for in our daily tasks, is that the REACH dimensions are within our grasp.

H for Health

And just one final message of encouragement, expressed in the poem entitled, **The Gift**.

The Gift

Life should be a treasured gift, respected by all for what it is.

An opportunity to thrive despite personal hardships, disappointments and trials, and the challenges that seem unfair that make life at times so difficult to bear.

But our bodies and minds were given to enjoy through emotions, communications, creativity and more.

Sights and sounds great joys revealing, and where touch, taste and smell can enhance our feelings.

But the gift wasn't given so that just we alone could exist, its purpose was for all of mankind to experience love and respect.

Not least, for ourselves to achieve what we dare, and to share our good fortunes with others out there.

And let's not forget our home, planet Earth, a place of beauty, variety, great wonder and worth.

It's here we exist, because life is a gift, to engage in the human experience, which we could so easily have missed.

To have not been conceived is difficult to imagine, and not existing at all, is almost impossible to fathom.

So, treasure the gift, your experiences, your being, even though life as you see it may not be quite to your pleasing.

Let's talk REACH

Because whilst the journey of life has its twists and its turns, we can change its direction, if we are willing to learn.

And remember, unlike a gift that we might receive, for example, as a **birthday present** – which is likely to have **a specific purpose** and **limited use** – life is **a dynamic gift**; a gift **that provides endless possibilities**, within our **R**, **E**, **A**, **C** and **H** dimensions.

And since the way we think, and what we think about, affects the way we feel, and the way we feel **has the potential to affect our behaviours**, then **thinking differently** and expressing our feelings with love, care, consideration and respect, is so important. It is important (as we have discussed), not only for our own well-being, but for the well-being of those with whom we relate.

If therefore, you have been inspired by any of the seventy poems in this book, or our conversations that might have, or could have a **positive impact** on your life, or someone else's life, that would be fantastic. And, as suggested in the last line of the above poem, we can, **if we are willing to learn**, change the direction of our journey through life, if we choose to:

… whilst the journey of life has its twists and its turns, we can change its direction, if we are willing to learn.

I have really enjoyed our conversation, and we may speak again soon.

Bye for now.

What we have talked about

Poems in green text with brief explanatory notes.

Introduction
About this book 1, 2
Basic ingredients of human life 1, 2
Introduction to the poems 3
Life Is (An adventure and a challenge) 3
Taking control 4
The way we think, and what we think about, affects the way we feel. 4
It's in the Mind (Thoughts; sensations in the mind) 5
Forethought; the conscious and unconscious mind 6
The purpose of our conversation 6

R for Relationships
Introduction 7
Relationships (Concerning their purpose) 7. 8
Relationship failure 8
Loneliness (Loss and distress when a friendship ends) 8, 9
The importance of companionship 9
Self-awareness 9 – 11
First Thoughts (Life dictates how thoughts are formed) 13
Ingrained experiences, memories and emotions 14
Childhood experiences 14 – 16
Childhood Memories (The good, and the not so good) 14, 15
The potential consequences of childhood experiences 16
Is Life Fair? (Considering one's lot in life) 16
Despair – a destructive element 17

Let's talk REACH

Role of the subconscious mind 17

The ability to think for ourselves 18

Mislead (A time to reassess) 18

Self-analysis and self-awareness 18, 19

Critical Disclosure (Self-awareness and emotional intelligence) 19

Self-awareness and emotional intelligence discussion 19 – 23

Self-awareness (Its importance, role and value) 22, 23

Minds paralysis 23 - 25

Communication, Compassion, Compromise, Commitment 23

Empathy Revealed (An explanation) 25

Knowing ourselves 26

Being Myself (Questioning one's attitude towards patience and intolerance) 28

Uniqueness (Opinions that reflect a self-centred perspective) 29, 30

Intolerance and its consequences 30

Romantic Relationships (Respect and compromise) 30, 31

Internet dating 31

Disillusioned Dater (Let's give it a go, one more time) 31, 32

A degree of attraction 32, 33

Relationships have a purpose 33 - 35

Romantic Ties (Hoped for and responsibilities requirements) 34

Inner beauty; the desire to be with characteristic 35, 36

Patience and intolerance 36

Impatient; That's Me (An unfortunate state of mind) 36

Impatience where it matters 36, 37

Patience or What? (Taking all into consideration) 37, 38

Impatience Demands (But doesn't always achieve the desired outcome) 38

Patience where it matters 39

Bullying, racism, sexism, domestic abuse – introduction 40

What we have talked about

Bullying 40 - 45

It's What I Am (A perspective on bullying) 41, 42

Bullying in different locations 42 - 45

Feelings (Supporting a friend who is being bullied) 43, 44

Bullying helpline contact details 45

Racism; definition and psychological theories 45 – 48

I'm a Racist (An individual's racist's thought processes and reflections) 46

Racism can damage the racist mental health 48

Darkness Revealed (A challenge to the perceptions of racism) 49, 50

The getting to know someone process 50

Sexism; definition and discussion 51

The Great Revealing (The growing up years) 52

Maturity; unlocking the sense of responsibility 52

Sexism Experienced (A young woman expresses her feelings to her abuser) 53, 54

Discussing sexist behaviour and an alien invasion 54, 55

Domestic abuse; definition, examples and support 55, 56

Silent Thoughts (Working out in a domestic abuse situation, how to proceed) 56

Being abused as a disabled person 57

My Disabilities (Suffering and abuse) 57

Abuse takes many different forms 58

Disabilities Uncovered (When not being a 'decent human being', could be considered a disability) 58, 59

Fraudsters and criminals of every kind 59, 60

Pressing the pause button 60

E for enjoyment

Introduction 61

Enjoyment; a positive emotional and physical response 61

161

Let's talk REACH

The Enjoyment Factor (Some of the 'mechanisms' of enjoyment) 61, 62
A state of mind 62
Personality 63
People who make life more enjoyable 63
Self-awareness and emotional intelligence 64
Excuses (Attitudes that can elude our achieving) 66
Overcoming our fears 66, 67
Lack of confidence and emotional detachment 68, 69
The Duck (The desire to be interested) 70
Becoming less boring! 71
Observing other people 71
Tell Me (Why are you so confident?) 72
Having a belief in yourself 72
Enjoyment through creativity 72, 73
Patience Matters (When being patient can be beneficial) 73
Impatient behaviour 74
What Right? (Challenging self-importance) 74
Do we have a right to be impatient? 74, 75
Enjoyment in creative tasks 75
It's OK (Enjoyment; search out your entitlement) 76
Respecting and caring 76
Joint Attraction (The importance of mutual satisfaction) 77
Feeling low or struggling: seek help 78

A for Achievement
Introduction 79
Determination (Overcoming set-backs) 79, 80
Sometimes just making the effort is what's required. 80
And the ask yourself; Are you sure? 80

What we have talked about

Are You Sure? (Challenging old perceptions) 81
The achievement journey 81, 82
Thinking differently 82
Achievement Happens (When thinking differently has arrived) 82
Try to think differently. The survival of planet Earth 83
The Planet Speaks (But are we listening) 83
Overproduction, overconsumption, use and disposal of products 84
Economic Growth (What' it all about, GDP?) 84, 85
The mess we are in 85, 86
Implications (To buy or not to buy; that is the question) 87
Considering our purchases 87
It's Not Unreasonable (Why should I be deprived) 88
Fairness and equality 89, 90
Past failures, missed opportunities, or just bad luck 89, 90
I'm a Loser (Sad perceptions) 89
What could go wrong? 89, 90
It's My Fault (Unjustified self-criticism) 90
Breaking free from the clutches of self-doubt 91 - 93
Feeling better 92, 93
Let's Be Clear (Life on Earth; a matter of balance) 93, 94
Survival of the Planet 95, 96
Success in the mind does not always have to relate to possessions 96, 97

C for Comfort

Introduction 98
Comfort Pains (In the body and in the mind) 98
Comfort/discomfort experiences 99 - 101
The Comfort Journey (Promoting the human existence and its deliverance) 101, 102

Let's talk REACH

A responsibility of the highest stake 102, 103

Comfort Beckons (And is derived through mutual satisfaction) 103, 104

Thinking differently 104

Does it Matter (For the disheartened yes, let your old life no longer matter) 104, 105

Comfort derived from different situations 106, 107

The Comfort Zone (Closing the door on the restrictive comfort zone) 107, 108

Lack of confidence, fear of the unknown 108

Self-imposed discomfort 108

A Peaceful Mind (Where comfort thrives) 108, 109

Over-reacting unnecessarily 110 - 111

The impact of comfort on our R, E, A. C and H experiences 111, 112

H for Health

Introduction 113

The Body (A structure that should demand our deepest respect) 113, 114

Getting a level of comprehension 114

Breathing (Good clean air is all that we actually require) 114, 115

The dangers of smoking and vaping 115 - 118

Other drugs abuse 118

Viruses 118

Talking about food 118 - 124

It Tastes Good (The digestive system; it's not a pleasure garden) 119

Food groups 120 - 124

Food labels and GDA 120

Poor diet and health conditions 124

Alcoholic Drinks (An accepted part of social entertainment – but it excess, it can become a liability) 124, 125

Affects of alcohol on health and safety 125, 126

Mental health; what is it? 126

What we have talked about

Mind Teaser (Conversations in the mind) 127

Self-doubt, fretting, regretting 128

Categories of human activity 129, 130

Ask Yourself (Do you really know yourself?) 131, 132

Thoughts and their effect on mental health 132

Anxiety (Disturbing a peaceful mind) 132, 133

Calming a troubled mind 133, 134

Depression 134

Depressed - Or What? (Am I depressed?) 135

Depression; symptoms, specialist help 135

Sleep issues, hoarding, gambling 136 -142

I Can't Sleep (Everything going round and round) 137

The National Sleep Helpline website 137

Hording 137

Hoarding (Do I see things differently to how others can) 138, 139

Gambling 139 - 141

Confessions of a Reformed Gambler (How it all started) 141, 142

Exercise 142, 144

The basis ingredients of human life 144

REACH: The Indisputable Connections (Comfort at the heart) 145, 146

Seeing the whole picture 147, 148

Why, What, When? (The sorting out process) 149

Comfort as the driving force 148 - 150

Comfort Matters (Positivity and harmony) 150, 151

The comfort spectrum 151, 152

Thinking differently 152, 153

Patience and tolerance 153

Impatience Can (The health connection) 154

Impatience and our R, E, C, and H 154, 155

Let's talk REACH

Better Times (Where patient thoughts decisions make) 155, 156

The way we react communicate and behave 156

The REACH Dimensions (Bringing it to a conclusion) 156

The Gift (An opportunity the thrive) 157, 158

Concluding thoughts 158